Primary Source Fluency Activities
Expanding & Preserving the Union

Introduction by
Dr. Timothy Rasinski

Author

Wendy Conklin, M.A.

Special Introduction by

Dr. Timothy Rasinski, Kent State University

Shell Educational Publishing

Editorial Project Manager
Emily R. Smith, M.A. Ed.

Editor-in-Chief
Sharon Coan, M.S. Ed.

Art Director
Lee Aucoin

Cover Art
The Library of Congress
Photodisc

Imaging
Alfred Lau

Production Manager
Phil Garcia

Publisher
Corinne Burton, M.S. Ed.

Shell Educational Publishing
5301 Oceanus Drive
Huntington Beach, CA 92649-1030
www.seppub.com
ISBN-0-7439-8187-1
©2006 Shell Educational Publishing
Made in U.S.A.
Reprinted, 2006

Table of Contents

Table of Contents *(cont.)*

Introduction to Teaching Fluency

By Dr. Timothy Rasinski
Kent State University

Why This Book?

This book was developed in response to the need we have heard from teachers for good texts for teaching reading fluency within the content areas. Within the past several years, reading fluency has become recognized as an essential element in elementary and middle grade reading programs (National Reading Panel, 2001). Readers who are fluent are better able to comprehend what they read—they decode words so effortlessly that they can devote their cognitive resources to the all-important task of comprehension instead of bogging themselves down in working to decode words they confront in their reading. They can also construct meaning (comprehension) by reading with appropriate expression and phrasing.

Readers develop fluency through guided practice and repeated readings—reading a text selection several times to the point where it can be expressed meaningfully— with appropriate expression and phrasing. Readers who engage in regular repeated readings, under the guidance and assistance of a teacher or other coach, improve their word recognition, reading rate, comprehension, and overall reading proficiency.

Students will find the texts in this book interesting and sometimes challenging. Students will especially want to practice the texts if you provide regular opportunities for them to perform the texts for their classmates, parents, and other audiences.

So, have fun with these passages. Read them with your students and read them again. Be assured that if you regularly have your students read and perform the texts in this book, you will go a long way to develop fluent readers who are able to decode words effortlessly and construct meaning through their interpretations of texts.

How to Use This Book

The texts in this book are meant to be read, reread, and performed. If students do this, they will develop as fluent readers—improve their ability to recognize words accurately and effortlessly and read with meaningful expression and phrasing. However, you, the teachers, are the most important part in developing instruction that uses these texts. In this section, we recommend ways in which you can use the texts with your students.

Scheduling and Practice

The texts should be read repeatedly over several days. We recommend that you introduce one text at a time and practice it over the next three, four, or five days, depending on how quickly your students develop mastery over them. Write the text you are going to read on chart paper and/or put it on an overhead transparency.

Have the students read the text several times each day. They should read it a couple times at the beginning of each day; read it several times during various breaks in the day; and read it multiple times at the end of each day.

Make two copies of the text for each student. Have students keep one copy in school in their "fluency folders." The other copy can be sent home for the students to continue practicing with their families. Communicate to families the importance of children continuing to practice the text at home with their parents and other family members.

Coaching Your Students

A key ingredient to repeated reading is the coaching that comes from a teacher. As your students practice reading the target text each week, alone, in small groups, or as an entire class, be sure to provide positive feedback about their reading. Help them develop a sense for reading the text in such a way that it conveys the meaning that the author attempts to convey or the meaning that the reader may wish to convey. Through oral interpretation of a text, readers can express joy, sadness, anger, surprise, or any of a variety of emotions. Help students learn to use their reading to convey this level of meaning.

Teachers do this by listening, from time to time, as students read and coaching them in the various aspects of oral interpretation. You may wish to suggest that students emphasize certain words, insert dramatic pauses, read a bit faster in one place, or slow down in other parts of the text. And, of course, lavish praise on students' best efforts to convey a sense of meaning through their reading. Although it may take a while for the students to learn to develop this sense of "voice" in their reading, in the long run, it will lead to more engaged and fluent reading and higher levels of comprehension.

Introduction to Teaching Fluency *(cont.)*
By Dr. Timothy Rasinski

Word Study

Although the goal of the passages in this book is to develop fluent and meaningful oral reading, the practicing of passages should also provide opportunities to develop students' vocabulary and word decoding skills. Students may practice a passage repeatedly to the point where it is largely memorized. At this point, students may not look at the words in the text as closely as they ought. By continually drawing attention to interesting and important words in the text, you can help students maintain their focus and develop an ongoing fascination with words.

After reading a passage several times through, ask students to choose words from the passage that they think are interesting or important. Put these words on a word wall, or ask students to add them to their personal word banks. Talk about the words—their meanings and spellings. Help students develop a deepened appreciation for these words. Encourage students to use these words in their oral and written language. You might, for example, ask students to use some of the chosen words in their daily journal entries.

Once a list of words has been added to a classroom word wall or students' word banks, play various games with the words. One of our favorites is "word bingo." Here, students are given a card containing a 3 x 3, 4 x 4, or 5 x 5 grid. In each box, students randomly write words from the word wall or bank. Then, the teacher calls out words or sentences that contain the target words or definitions of the target words. Students find the words on their cards and cover them with markers. Once a horizontal, vertical, or diagonal line of words is covered, a student calls "Bingo" and wins the game.

Have students sort the chosen words along a variety of dimensions—by syllable, part of speech, presence of a certain phonics features such as long vowel sound or a consonant blend, or by meaning (e.g., words that express how a person can feel and words that don't). Through sorting-and-categorizing activities, students get repeated exposure to words, examining the words differently with each sort.

Choose words from a text that lend themselves to extended word family instruction. Choose a word like "hat" and brainstorm with students other words that belong to the same word family (e.g., cat, bat, and chat). Once a brainstormed list of word family words are chosen, have students create short poems using the rhyming words. These composed poems can be used for further practice and performance.

No matter how you do it, make the opportunity to examine selected words from the passages part of your regular instructional routine for these fluency texts. The time spent in word study will most definitely improve students' overall fluency.

Introduction to Teaching Fluency (cont.)
By Dr. Timothy Rasinski

Performance

After several days of practice, arrange a special time for the students to perform the text, as well as other ones practiced from previous days. This performance time can range from 5 minutes to 30 minutes. Find a special person (such as the principal) to listen to your children perform. You may also want to invite a neighboring class, parents, or another group to come to your room to listen to your children perform. Have the children perform the targeted text as a group. Later, you can have individuals or groups of children perform the text again, as well as other texts that have been practiced previously.

As an alternative to having your children perform for a group that comes to your room, you may also want to send your children to visit other adults and children in the building and perform for them. Principals, school secretaries, custodians, playground aides, and visitors to the building are usually great audiences for children's readings. Tape recording and video taping your students' readings is another way to create a performance opportunity.

Regardless of how you do it, it is important that you create the opportunity for your students to perform for some audience. The magic of the performance will give students the motivation to want to practice their assigned texts.

Performance Not Memorization

Remember that the key to developing fluency is guided oral and silent reading practice. Students become more fluent when they read the texts repeatedly. Reading requires students to actually see the words in the texts. Thus, it is important that you do not require students to memorize the texts they are practicing and performing. Memorization leads students away from visually examining the words. Although students may want to try to memorize some texts, the instructional emphasis needs to be on reading with expression so that any audience will enjoy the students' oral renderings of the texts. Keep students' eyes on the texts whenever possible.

One of the most important things we can do to promote proficient and fluent reading is to have students practice reading meaningful passages with a purpose: to perform them. This program provides students with just those opportunities to create meaning with their voices as well as the wonderful words in these primary sources.

How to Use This Product

General Information

This book contains famous historical texts such as speeches, poems, letters, government documents, newspaper articles, and songs. Each of these primary sources is from America in the 1800s (i.e., the Louisiana Purchase through the Civil War and into the Indian conflicts in the 1880s). Activities for each primary source teach important fluency strategies while covering key historical events and people, such as exploring the Louisiana Purchase, American Indian tribes, pioneer life, the Civil War Era, James Madison, Sitting Bull, Abraham Lincoln, and Ulysses S. Grant.

Depending on the reading levels of your students, you may find some of these pieces too difficult to use at the beginning of the year. Instead, focus on the pieces that are rewritten or pieces where the original reading level is lower. Unfortunately for students today, we write differently now than the people of the past. What that means for our students is that they often have to decipher very difficult and complex writing just to read a primary source document. This book is set up to help your students be successful as they tackle writings from the past. Instead of just reading the document or letter once and moving on, the students practice and reread the pieces in preparation for authentic presentations. That way, not only does their fluency grow through careful repetition, but as the class discusses the pieces, the students' comprehension improves as well.

Presentations

One of the most important aspects of these lessons are the presentation pieces. The author and editors of this book have tried to provide you with plenty of ideas. If the idea suggested for a certain piece will not work for your classroom situation, flip through the book and look for other suggestions that might be suitable. The key is that you have the students practice reading the pieces for authentic reasons. If the end presentations are always just to their own classes, students will quickly lose interest. Once they've lost interest in the performance, they will not work as hard at perfecting their fluency. You will not see much growth in your students if they feel that all their practice is for nothing.

Instead, be creative and fun as you plan these presentations. Invite different guests or whole classes in to hear your presentations. Younger classes make great audiences if the content is something they are also studying. Keep in mind that many teachers of younger students cover Laura Ingalls Wilder, Abraham Lincoln, Lewis and Clark, American Indians, and the Civil War whether it is specifically in their standards or not.

How to Use This Product *(cont.)*

Presentations *(cont.)*

If you have a hard time finding people to whom your class can present, try to tie the presentations into celebrations or holidays. Some possible times to hold presentations might include: Presidents' Day, the beginning of spring, Mother's Day, Memorial Day, Flag Day, the first day of summer, Father's Day, Labor Day, the beginning of autumn, Columbus Day, Election Day, Veteran's Day, Thanksgiving Day, and the first day of winter. Don't forget about celebrations that take place over whole months. Some of these include: Black History Month, American Indian Heritage Month, and Women's History Month.

Finally, try to tie your presentations into schoolwide events. For example, you could have your students add to the school's morning announcements. Or, you could ask for a special part in the Veteran's Day celebration. Rather than holding your own assembly, work with other teachers to hold a Poetry Celebration where students read historical poetry. Remember, your students' fluency will only improve if you make the performances important and authentic.

Reader's Theater

Throughout the lessons in this book, you will find numerous reader's theater scripts. This is an exciting and easy method of providing students with the opportunity to practice fluency leading to a performance. Because reader's theater minimizes the use of props, sets, costumes, and memorization, it is an easy way to present a "play" in the classroom. Students read from a book or prepared script using their voices to bring text to life. Reader's theater has the following characteristics:

1. The script is always read and never memorized.
2. Readers may be characters, narrators, or switch back and forth.
3. The readers may sit, stand, or both, but they do not have to perform any other actions.
4. Readers use only eye contact, facial expressions, and vocal expression to express emotion.
5. Scripts may be from books, songs, poems, letters, etc. They can be performed directly from the original material or adapted specifically for the reader's theater performance.
6. Musical accompaniment or soundtracks may be used but are not necessary.
7. Very simple props may be used, especially with younger children, to help the audience identify the roles played by the readers.
8. Practice for the reader's theater should consist of coached repeated readings that lead to a smooth, fluent presentation.

How to Use This Product *(cont.)*

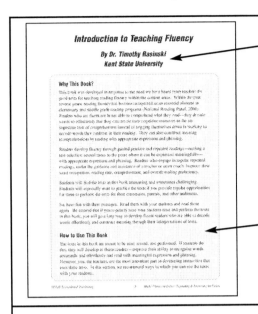

Introduction Written by Dr. Timothy Rasinski

- In a survey conducted by the National Reading Panel, fluency was determined to be one of the five research-based components of reading. Dr. Timothy Rasinski from Kent State University is an expert on teaching students to become fluent readers. His book, *The Fluent Reader*, is an excellent resource of oral reading strategies for building word recognition, fluency, and comprehension.

How to Use This Book

- Dr. Rasinski's introduction contains important information and ideas of how to use this book with your readers.

Objective

- A fluency objective is included for each lesson. This objective tells you which fluency strategy will be practiced within the lesson. See pages 13–14 for descriptions of the fluency strategies used within this book.

Fluency Suggestions and Activities

- These steps in the lesson plan describe how to introduce the piece to your students. Suggestions for ways to practice and perform the piece are also provided for your use. Remember that authentic performances are very important to ensure successful fluency for your readers.

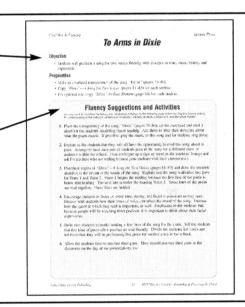

History Connection

- Each text in this book relates to an important historical person or event. Information is provided with each lesson to give you the historical context of the piece.

Vocabulary Connection

- Vocabulary words have been chosen and defined for your use. Introduce the words to your students and have them define the words or simply record the definitions on the board for student reference.

Extension Ideas

- One or two extension ideas are given for each lesson. These ideas are usually fun, challenging, and interesting.

How to Use This Product *(cont.)*

Primary Source Text

- For each lesson, a copy of the primary source text is provided for the teacher. Sometimes, the students will not receive copies of this text. They may only receive copies of the rewritten text, divided reading, or reader's theater. This text is provided so that teachers can read the original document to the students and/or refer to it as they teach the lesson to the class.

Student Versions of the Primary Source Text

- For most of the texts, the author of the book has rewritten the texts for the students to use. Sometimes, it is simply rephrased in modern language. Other times, the texts have been divided into smaller reading sections. There are also pieces that have been rewritten into reader's theater scripts for the students to perform.

Student Reproducibles

- For most of the lessons, at least one of the student reproducibles is designed to help students analyze the text. These are quite often one of the extension activities, since they do not focus on fluency as much as comprehension of the piece. If time allows, be sure to complete these activity sheets with your students.

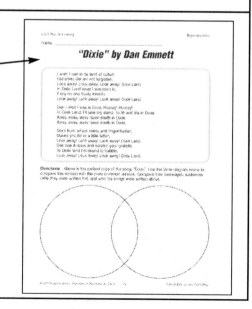

Fluency Strategy Descriptions

These paragraphs describe the fluency strategies taught through the lessons in this book. These descriptions are meant to provide teachers with basic information about the strategies before beginning the lessons.

Call and Response

Call and response is a type of choral reading. When using call and response, one student reads a portion of the text and then the class (or a group of students within the class) responds by reading the refrain, reading the next lines in the text, or repeating the same lines as the reader.

Choral Reading

Choral reading is when groups of students read the same text aloud together. It allows for a lot of reading time by all students rather than single students reading while everyone else listens.

Cumulative Choral Reading

This is a special type of choral reading where one student begins reading. Then, at predetermined points, other students join in the reading. By the end of the passage, the entire group is reading in unison.

Divided Reading

Divided reading is used when dealing with a large piece of text like a long speech, short story, or chapters in a book. The text is divided into parts and read over several days by groups of students.

Echo Reading

In echo reading, one reader (or a small group) reads a part of the text. Then, the rest of the group (or class) echoes back the same text.

Oral Reading

Oral reading is when the students read the text aloud rather than silently. All of the strategies in this book fall under the strategy of oral reading.

Paired Reading

Paired reading is when two students or a student and an adult read text together. They can either read it chorally, or they can read alternating lines or stanzas.

Poem or Song for Two Voices

This type of poem or song has been written (or rewritten) so that it can be read by two readers. The readers alternate between lines while sometimes reading lines together.

Reader's Theater

Reader's theater is usually written for three to five students. It includes lines of a text that are read individually and lines that are stated by all the students. It is like the script of a play, but there are few props and no costumes used in the production of the piece.

Repeated Reading

This type of reading is when the students read and reread a piece to improve upon their fluency. Every lesson within this book suggests that you have the students use repeated reading to improve their fluency before the performance of the piece.

Fluency Strategy Descriptions (cont.)

This chart indicates the fluency strategies practiced within the lessons in this book. Some lessons have more than one strategy marked because students will be working on multiple skills within the lesson.

	Call and Response	Choral Reading	Cumulative Choral Reading	Divided Reading	Echo Reading	Oral Reading	Paired Reading	Poem or Song for Two Voices	Reader's Theater	Repeated Reading
Beautiful America	x	x				x				x
My Country 'Tis of Thee		x	x			x				x
The National Anthem		x	x			x				x
Taking Up Arms						x	x			x
Waiting for the Pony Express						x			x	x
The Trip West	x					x				x
The Lady Who Started a War						x			x	x
Letting the Slaves Go	x					x				x
Surrendering at Last		x				x				x
Red Cloud Speaks				x		x				x
Abolitionists		x	x			x				x
To Arms in Dixie						x		x		x
Sherman's March					x	x				x
Following Jackson						x	x			x
Glory! Glory! Hallelujah!		x				x				x
Marching Home from War						x		x		x
Lewis's Adventures						x			x	x
Clark and His Men						x				x
Hailing the Chief						x		x		x
Mr. Madison's War						x		x		x
Little House Books				x		x				x
Pioneer Girl						x			x	x
A Song for Harriet					x	x				x
The Underground Railroad						x			x	x
Sitting Bull Speaks His Mind		x	x			x				x
A Definition of a Warrior	x					x				x
Addressing Freedom						x			x	x
The Captain!						x			x	x
Lee and the Civil War	x					x				x
Saying Farewell						x			x	x
The Warrior Grant				x		x				x
In Grant's Own Words				x		x				x

Beautiful America

Objective

√ Students will read "America the Beautiful" using the call-and-response method.

Preparation

- Make an overhead transparency of the poem, "America the Beautiful" (page 17).
- Copy *"America the Beautiful"—Call and Response* (page 18) for each student.

Fluency Suggestions and Activities

You may want to complete the history and vocabulary activities on the following page before starting this fluency activity. An understanding of the historical context and vocabulary will help students analyze and read the piece fluently.

Note: You might want to plan to complete this fluency activity on September 11 to remember those who died in the 2001 terrorist attacks.

1. Begin by asking students to name the national anthem of the United States. Some students might think the national anthem is "America the Beautiful." Be sure to point out that many people in the United States believe this or think it should be true. However, the official national anthem is "The Star Spangled Banner" (see lesson on pages 23–26). Some people call "America the Beautiful" the *other* national anthem.

2. Place a transparency of the poem, "America the Beautiful" (page 17), on the overhead and read it aloud, modeling fluent reading for the students.

3. Give each student a copy of *"America the Beautiful"—Call and Response* (page 18) and read it aloud together (choral reading) several times. Model reading lines with changes in pitch, tone, and timing to achieve different effects. Although this is a song, you are treating it like a poem. It'll be hard not to break into song. Feel free to sing if you are musically talented!

4. Tell students that one group of them will be reading this song on the intercom for the entire student body.

5. Place students into groups of eight to read the song together using *"America the Beautiful"—Call and Response.* Allow time for the students to practice the song several times. You may want to play recorded copies of the song for the students as well during this practice period.

6. When all the groups feel prepared, have them perform a reading of this song for the class. The class can decide which group of eight students should represent the class on the school intercom. (You may decide that this poem is too long to be read in one day. You could have students read the poem in different small groups throughout the week. They could read one or two stanzas per day. This would also allow you to have more students participate in the actual performance.)

Beautiful America (cont.)

History Connection

Introduce "America the Beautiful" using the information provided below.

Katherine Lee Bates, a teacher, visited Pike's Peak in Colorado in 1893 with a group of fellow teachers. They hired a prairie wagon to take them there. Close to the top of the peak, they had to leave the wagon behind and ride the rest of the way on mules. She was so inspired by the beautiful scenery at the top of the peak that she said, "All the wonder of America seemed displayed there, with the sea-like expanse." She wrote a poem about her experience titled, "America the Beautiful." Two years later, it appeared in print for others to read. Different kinds of folk music were used to sing this poem. One of the favorite tunes was "Auld Lang Syne." Katherine revised her poem two times, changing the words and in 1910, the words were published with the tune that people sing today.

Vocabulary Connection

Discuss unfamiliar vocabulary encountered in the text. Some possible words are listed below. After identifying the difficult words, discuss them within the context of the text.

- **spacious**—having lots of space or room
- **amber**—a brownish-yellow color
- **impassioned**—having a strong or passionate feeling
- **thoroughfare**—a passageway
- **liberating strife**—a fight for freedom
- **alabaster**—whitish color used for statues
- **halcyon**—calm or peaceful
- **enameled**—colorful
- **lavished**—gave generously
- **nobler**—showing great character

Extension Idea

- Have students interview people in their neighborhoods and in the school to gather public sentiment about which song makes a better national anthem: "America the Beautiful" or "The Star Spangled Banner." They should have copies of the lyrics of both songs on hand to let their interviewees read. Let students present the information they have gathered to the class. Then, take a vote within the class about the issue.

America the Beautiful

By Katherine Lee Bates

O beautiful for spacious skies,
For amber waves of grain,
For purple mountain majesties
Above the fruited plain!
America! America!
God shed his grace on thee
And crown thy good with brotherhood
From sea to shining sea!

O beautiful for pilgrim feet
Whose stern impassioned stress
A thoroughfare for freedom beat
Across the wilderness!
America! America!
God mend thine every flaw,
Confirm thy soul in self-control,
Thy liberty in law!

O beautiful for heroes proved
In liberating strife.
Who more than self their country loved
And mercy more than life!
America! America!
May God thy gold refine
Till all success be nobleness
And every gain divine!

O beautiful for patriot dream
That sees beyond the years
Thine alabaster cities gleam
Undimmed by human tears!
America! America!
God shed his grace on thee
And crown thy good with brotherhood
From sea to shining sea!

O beautiful for halcyon skies,
For amber waves of grain,
For purple mountain majesties
Above the enameled plain!
America! America!
God shed his grace on thee
Till souls wax fair as earth and air
And music-hearted sea!

O beautiful for pilgrims feet,
Whose stern impassioned stress
A thoroughfare for freedom beat
Across the wilderness!
America! America!
God shed his grace on thee
Till paths be wrought through
    wilds of thought
By pilgrim foot and knee!

O beautiful for glory-tale
Of liberating strife
When once and twice,
For man's avail
Men lavished precious life!
America! America!
God shed his grace on thee
Till selfish gain no longer stain
The banner of the free!

O beautiful for patriot dream
That sees beyond the years
Thine alabaster cities gleam
Undimmed by human tears!
America! America!
God shed his grace on thee
Till nobler men keep once again
Thy whiter jubilee!

Name _____

"America the Beautiful"—Call and Response

R1: O beautiful for spacious skies,
For amber waves of grain,
For purple mountain majesties
Above the fruited plain!

All: **America! America!**
God shed his grace on thee
And crown thy good with
brotherhood
From sea to shining sea!

R2: O beautiful for pilgrim feet
Whose stern impassioned stress
A thoroughfare for freedom beat
Across the wilderness!

All: **America! America!**
God mend thine every flaw,
Confirm thy soul in self-control,
Thy liberty in law!

R3: O beautiful for heroes proved
In liberating strife.
Who more than self their country loved
And mercy more than life!

All: **America! America!**
May God thy gold refine
Till all success be nobleness
And every gain divine!

R4: O beautiful for patriot dream
That sees beyond the years
Thine alabaster cities gleam
Undimmed by human tears!

All: **America! America!**
God shed his grace on thee
And crown thy good with
brotherhood
From sea to shining sea!

R5: O beautiful for halcyon skies,
For amber waves of grain,
For purple mountain majesties
Above the enameled plain!

All: **America! America!**
God shed his grace on thee
Till souls wax fair as earth
and air
And music-hearted sea!

R6: O beautiful for pilgrims feet,
Whose stern impassioned
stress
A thoroughfare for freedom
beat
Across the wilderness!

All: **America! America!**
God shed his grace on thee
Till paths be wrought through
wilds of thought
By pilgrim foot and knee!

R7: O beautiful for glory-tale
Of liberating strife
When once and twice,
For man's avail
Men lavished precious life!

All: **America! America!**
God shed his grace on thee
Till selfish gain no longer
stain
The banner of the free!

R8: O beautiful for patriot dream
That sees beyond the years
Thine alabaster cities gleam
Undimmed by human tears!

All: **America! America!**
God shed his grace on thee
Till nobler men keep once
again
Thy whiter jubilee!

My Country 'Tis of Thee

Objective

√ Students will read passages fluently and accurately within a cumulative choral-reading activity, focusing on using correct conversational and expressive language.

Preparation

- Make an overhead transparency of the song, "America" (page 21).
- Copy *"America"—Cumulative Choral Reading* (page 22) for each student.

Fluency Suggestions and Activities

You may want to complete the history and vocabulary activities on the following page before starting this fluency activity. An understanding of the historical context and vocabulary will help students analyze and read the piece fluently.

1. Ask students if they know the title of the song that begins with the following line, "My country, 'tis of thee." Most students might think this line is also the title, or they might confuse this song with "America the Beautiful." Clarify to students that this song is called "America."

2. Read the lyrics of "America" (page 21) by Samuel Francis Smith aloud, modeling fluent reading. Tell students that they will be reading this song in front of different classrooms in the school.

3. Explain to students that they will read "America" as a cumulative choral reading. Divide students into groups of four and distribute copies of the *"America"—Cumulative Choral Reading* (page 22). This sheet has the first four stanzas of the song on it.

4. Assign each student in each group a part to read. Explain that R1, R2, R3, and R4 stand for Reader 1, Reader 2, Reader 3, and Reader 4. Draw their attention to the way a new reader is added on each line—first one reader, then two, then three, and then four reading together at the same time. Then, one by one, each reader stops reading until the original reader is left reading the passage. Demonstrate this process with student volunteers using the stanza (shown below).

R1:	My country, 'tis of Thee,
R1, R2:	Sweet Land of Liberty,
R1, R2, R3:	Of thee I sing;
R1, R2, R3, R4:	Land where my fathers died,
R1, R2, R3:	Land of the pilgrim's pride,
R1, R2:	From ev'ry mountain side
R1:	Let Freedom ring.

5. Have the students discuss words or phrases that should carry particular expressive emphasis. Then, be sure you allow students time in class to practice their cumulative readings of the text.

6. Arrange ahead of time to have each group present their reading to another class in the school.

My Country 'Tis of Thee (cont.)

History Connection

Introduce "My Country 'Tis of Thee" using the information provided below.

As a seminary student, Samuel Francis Smith wrote the poem, "America" in 1831. "America" was first sung at a July Fourth celebration for children in Boston. Soon, it was sung all throughout the nation. Most know this song as "My Country 'Tis of Thee," and many refer to it as the great national hymn of the United States.

Vocabulary Connection

Discuss unfamiliar vocabulary encountered in the text. Some possible words are listed below. After identifying the difficult words, discuss them within the context of the text.

- **native**—original, where someone was born
- **rills**—small brooks or creeks
- **rapture**—joy
- **mortal**—human
- **partake**—to share or take part

Extension Ideas

- Samuel Francis Smith wrote an additional verse that referred to Great Britain. He later took out the verse. Have students conduct research to find that missing verse and then analyze why Smith decided to take it out of the song.

- Many believe the words and music of "America" are inspiring. As students read and listen to the music of "America," have them draw pictures of the images they see in their minds. Place these on display for all to admire.

America

By Samuel Francis Smith

My country, 'tis of Thee,
Sweet Land of Liberty,
Of thee I sing;
Land where my fathers died,
Land of the pilgrims' pride,
From ev'ry mountain side
Let Freedom ring.

My native country, thee,
Land of the noble free,
Thy name I love;
I love thy rocks and rills,
Thy woods and templed hills;
My heart with rapture thrills
Like that above.

Let music swell the breeze,
And ring from all the trees
Sweet Freedom's song;
Let mortal tongues awake;
Let all that breathe partake;
Let rocks their silence break,
The sound prolong.

Our fathers' God to Thee,
Author of liberty,
To thee we sing,
Long may our land be bright
With Freedom's holy light
Protect us by thy might,
Great God, our King.

Name _____

"America"—
Cumulative Choral Reading

Directions: Read aloud your assigned part with the group.

R1:	My country, 'tis of Thee,
R1, R2:	Sweet Land of Liberty,
R1, R2, R3:	Of thee I sing;
R1, R2, R3, R4:	**Land where my fathers died,**
R1, R2, R3:	Land of the pilgrims' pride,
R1, R2:	From every mountain side,
R1:	Let Freedom ring.
R2:	My native country, thee,
R2, R3:	Land of the noble free,
R2, R3, R4:	Thy name I love;
R2, R3, R4, R1:	**I love thy rocks and rills,**
R2, R3, R4:	Thy woods and templed hills;
R2, R3:	My heart with rapture thrills
R2:	Like that above.
R3:	Let music swell the breeze,
R3, R4:	And ring from all the trees
R3, R4, R1:	Sweet Freedom's song;
R3, R4, R1, R2:	**Let mortal tongues awake;**
R3, R4, R1:	Let all that breathe partake;
R3, R4:	Let rocks their silence break,
R3:	The sound prolong.
R4:	Our fathers' God to Thee,
R4, R1:	Author of liberty,
R4, R1, R2:	To thee we sing,
R4, R1, R2, R3:	**Long my our land be bright,**
R4, R1, R2:	With Freedom's holy light,
R4, R1:	Protect us by thy might,
R4:	Great God, our King.

The National Anthem

Objective

√ Students will read passages fluently and accurately within a cumulative choral-reading activity, focusing on using correct conversational and expressive language.

Preparation

- Make an overhead transparency of the song, "The Star Spangled Banner" (page 25).
- Copy *"The Star Spangled Banner"—Cumulative Choral Reading* (page 26) for each student.

Fluency Suggestions and Activities

You may want to complete the history and vocabulary activities on the following page before starting this fluency activity. An understanding of the historical context and vocabulary will help students analyze and read the piece fluently.

1. Ask students to imagine they are at a sporting event, such as a baseball game or football game. See if the students know what famous song is sung before the event. Many students might know that it is "The Star Spangled Banner." See if any of the students can recite the first verse from memory. If not, recite it for them. Students might be surprised to learn that there are three more verses in the song.

2. Display the transparency of the song, "The Star Spangled Banner" (page 25), on the overhead projector for all to see. Read the first stanza, demonstrating fluency with accuracy and expression. Focus particular attention on the use of long sentences, divided by commas. Explain that when reading long sentences, it is important to pause when commas are encountered to assist with the understanding of the text. Focus on the sentences that end with a question mark, too. Use voice inflection to show that the sentences are questions. Then, have the students read the lyrics aloud together.

3. Explain to the students that they are practicing this skill so that they will be prepared for a group cumulative choral-reading activity. This reading activity is to celebrate the beginning of baseball season and will be performed during lunch in the school cafeteria.

4. Divide the class into four groups (G1, G2, G3, and G4). Distribute copies of *"The Star Spangled Banner"—Cumulative Choral Reading* (page 26). This choral reading will go in reverse order. Everyone will read the first stanza. Then the first group will remain silent and groups two, three, and four will read the second stanza. Groups three and four will read the third stanza. Group four will complete the reading with the fourth stanza while the other groups are silent.

5. Have the class practice reading their parts, focusing on expressive, conversational language. Since groups three and four read more of the poem, you may want to put some of your more confident readers in those groups.

6. Arrange for students to perform their cumulative readings publicly in the school cafeteria to celebrate the kick-off of baseball season around the beginning of April.

The National Anthem *(cont.)*

History Connection

Discuss the "The Star Spangled Banner" and the history behind it using this information.

Most Americans are familiar with the national anthem. But many people don't realize that while it was written almost 200 years ago, it wasn't named the national anthem until 1931. "The Star Spangled Banner" was first written as a poem in 1814. A man named Francis Scott Key watched an attack on Fort McHenry in Baltimore, Maryland. At that time, Baltimore was the third largest city in the United States. British ships attacked the fort hoping to take over the entire city. The attack was intense, but the American commander at Fort McHenry refused to lower the flag. The British ships withdrew, defeated. The next morning, Key saw the flag flying over the fort and it inspired him to write these words as a poem. By 1814, the poem had been put to music.

Vocabulary Connection

Discuss unfamiliar vocabulary encountered in the text. Some possible words are listed below. After identifying the difficult words, discuss them within the context of the text.

- **hail'd**—hailed; saluted or honored as being very special
- **perilous**—dangerous
- **ramparts**—the walls that encircle and protect people inside
- **gallantly**—bravely
- **haughty**—proud and arrogant
- **reposes**—waits and rests
- **discloses**—exposes; shows
- **vauntingly**—boastfully
- **havoc**—destruction
- **hireling**—someone hired to do work
- **desolation**—devastation or ruin

Extension Ideas

- Have students practice singing all the verses of "The Star Spangled Banner." If time allows, arrange for students to visit other classes and teach the other stanzas of the song.

- Encourage students to analyze the other stanzas in the poem. Why is only the first verse sung? Is it really the best one? Have the class poll students and teachers in the school to determine the best verse. Then, they can post the results on a school bulletin board or website.

The Star Spangled Banner

By Francis Scott Key

Oh say, can you see, by the dawn's early light,
What so proudly we hail'd at the twilight's last gleaming?
Whose broad stripes and bright stars, thro' the perilous fight,
O'er the ramparts we watch'd, were so gallantly streaming?
And the rockets' red glare, the bombs bursting in air,
Gave proof thro' the night that our flag was still there.
O say, does that star-spangled banner yet wave
O'er the land of the free and the home of the brave?

On the shore dimly seen thro' the mists of the deep,
Where the foe's haughty host in dread silence reposes,
What is that which the breeze, o'er the towering steep,
As it fitfully blows, half conceals, half discloses?
Now it catches the gleam of the morning's first beam,
In full glory reflected, now shines in the stream,
'Tis the star-spangled banner: O, long may it wave
O'er the land of the free and the home of the brave!

And where is that band who so vauntingly swore
That the havoc of war and the battle's confusion
A home and a country should leave us no more?
Their blood has wash'd out their foul footsteps' pollution.
No refuge could save the hireling and slave
From the terror of flight or the gloom of the grave:
And the star-spangled banner in triumph doth wave
O'er the land of the free and the home of the brave.

O thus be it ever when freemen shall stand,
Between their lov'd home and the war's desolation;
Blest with vict'ry and peace may the heav'n-rescued land
Praise the Pow'r that hath made and preserv'd us a nation!
Then conquer we must, when our cause it is just,
And this be our motto: "In God is our trust"
And the star-spangled banner in triumph shall wave
O'er the land of the free and the home of the brave!

Name _____

"The Star Spangled Banner"— Cumulative Choral Reading

G1, G2, G3, G4

Oh say, can you see, by the dawn's early light,

What so proudly we hailed at the twilight's last gleaming?

Whose broad stripes and bright stars through the perilous fight

O'er the ramparts we watched, were so gallantly streaming?

And the rockets' red glare, the bombs bursting in air,

Gave proof through the night that our flag was still there.

O say, does that star-spangled banner yet wave

O'er the land of the free and the home of the brave?

G2, G3, G4

On the shore dimly seen through the mists of the deep,

Where the foe's haughty host in dread silence reposes,

What is that which the breeze, o'er the towering steep,

As it fitfully blows, half conceals, half discloses?

Now it catches the gleam of the morning's first beam,

In full glory reflected, now shines in the stream,

'Tis the star-spangled banner: O, long may it wave

O'er the land of the free and the home of the brave!

G3, G4

And where is that band who so vauntingly swore

That the havoc of war and the battle's confusion

A home and a country should leave us no more?

Their blood has washed out their foul footsteps' pollution.

No refuge could save the hireling and slave

From the terror of flight or the gloom of the grave:

And the star-spangled banner in triumph doth wave

O'er the land of the free and the home of the brave.

G4

O, thus be it ever when freemen shall stand,

Between their loved home and the war's desolation;

Blest with vict'ry and peace may the heaven-rescued land

Praise the Power that hath made and preserved us a nation!

Then conquer we must, when our cause it is just,

And this be our motto: "In God is our trust"

And the star-spangled banner in triumph shall wave

O'er the land of the free and the home of the brave!

Taking Up Arms

Objective

√ Students will participate in paired-reading experiences, focusing on smooth reading, accuracy, reading rate, and expression.

Preparation

- Copy the song, "The Patriotic Diggers" (page 29), for each student.
- Make copies of *Assessing Fluency* (page 30) for the parent volunteers.
- Make copies of the *Fluency Chart* (page 31) for the parent volunteers.

Fluency Suggestions and Activities

You may want to complete the history and vocabulary activities on the following page before starting this fluency activity. An understanding of the historical context and vocabulary will help students analyze and read the piece fluently.

Note: You might want students to read this song close to Memorial Day or Veterans Day in honor of those who have served in the military.

1. Tell students that they will be reading a song about some men who served in the military during the War of 1812. Talk about the number of years between the American Revolution and the War of 1812. Ask students if they think the same men fought in both wars. If the men who fought in the Revolution were too old to fight, who fought in the War of 1812? It was most likely their sons.

2. Distribute copies of the song, "The Patriotic Diggers" (page 29). Read the lyrics aloud, modeling fluency. Ask students to listen for the clues of who is fighting in this war as you read.

3. Enlist the help of parent volunteers to complete a paired reading of the song. Provide each volunteer with copies of the reproducibles, *Assessing Fluency* (page 30) and *Fluency Chart* (page 31). *Assessing Fluency* describes the elements of fluency and explains how to complete the *Fluency Chart*.

4. Each student-parent pair should choose one stanza to read. When practicing, each parent and student should first read the text aloud together a few times. Encourage the parent to offer praise and suggestions as needed. Next, each student should read the text independently as the volunteer listens for the elements of fluency. In order not to distract the student, encourage the volunteer to complete the *Fluency Chart* after the paired-reading experience has ended.

5. Invite some guests who have served in the military to come hear a reading of this song from the War of 1812. Have students explain the background information about this song to their guests. Then, have reading pairs perform the song.

Taking Up Arms (cont.)

History Connection

Introduce "The Patriotic Diggers" using the information provided below.

This song was written by Samuel Woodworth in 1812 to honor the men who took up their arms to defend America against the British. They were called patriotic diggers because they were the ones breaking the soil of their new country. They were the laborers who made the country successful. These men were common citizens who believed in the independence their fathers had won during the Revolutionary War. Now, it was time for these sons to defend that liberty.

Vocabulary Connection

Discuss unfamiliar vocabulary encountered in the text. Some possible words are listed below. After identifying the difficult words, discuss them within the context of the text.

- **basting**—beating
- **flint and triggers**—ammunition and guns
- **yonder**—distant
- **ardently**—eagerly
- **marrow**—the spirit or heart
- **toil**—work
- **tabor**—a small drum
- **martial**—warlike
- **embattled**—under attack
- **concord**—peaceful

Extension Idea

- Allow students to conduct some additional research on the War of 1812. Ask students to work with partners to add another verse to the song. Have students analyze the following questions: How does their verse enhance the song? Does it explain more about the war at that time? Let students share their new verses with the class.

The Patriotic Diggers

By Samuel Woodworth

Enemies beware, keep a proper distance,
Else we'll make you stare at our firm resistance;
Let alone the lads who are freedom tasting,
Don't forget our dads gave you once a basting.
To protect our rights 'gainst your flint and triggers
See on yonder heights our patriotic diggers.
Men of ev'ry age, color, rank, profession,
Ardently engaged, labor in succession.
Pick-axe, shovel, spade, crow-bar, hoe and barrow
Better not invade, Yankees have the marrow.

Scholars leave their schools with patriotic teachers
Farmers seize their tools, headed by their preachers,
How they break the soil—brewers, butchers, bakers—
Here the doctors toil, there the undertakers.
Bright Apollo's sons leave their pipe and tabor,
Mid the roar of guns join the martial labor,
Round the embattled plain in sweet concord rally,
And in freedom's strain sing the foes finale.
Pick-axe, shovel, spade, crow-bar, hoe and barrow
Better not invade, Yankees have the marrow.

Better not invade, don't forget the spirit
Which our dads displayed and their sons inherit.
If you still advance, friendly caution slighting,
You may get by chance a bellyful of fighting!
Plumbers, founders, dyers, tinmen, turners, shavers,
Sweepers, clerks, and criers, jewelers and engravers,
Clothiers, drapers, players, cartmen, hatters, tailors,
Gaugers, sealers, weighers, carpenters and sailors!
Pick-axe, shovel, spade, crow-bar, hoe and barrow
Better not invade, Yankees have the marrow.

Assessing Fluency

Directions: Use the information below as you complete the *Fluency Chart* on page 31.

Passage: On these lines, record the name of the passage that the student read.

Smooth Reading: Listen as the student reads the passage. Pay attention to the manner in which he or she reads. Briefly respond to these questions.

- Does the student hesitate between words?
- Does the reading sound choppy?
- Does the student have a consistent pace when reading?

Reading Rates: The goal of fluency is not to read as quickly as possible, but rather to read at a comfortable pace. Listen as the student reads the passage.

- Does the student read at a rate that is pleasant to listen to and easy to comprehend?

Accuracy: As the student reads, pay attention to the number of mistakes made. The student should receive a positive comment if he or she is able to read with 80–90% accuracy. Students who receive below this may need some pointers about their common mistakes.

Expression: Part of fluent reading involves the ability to read with expression. This might involve varying the tone of voice when reading. This might also involve varying the sound of voice when different characters speak. As the student reads, consider the following questions:

- Does the student read in monotone?
- Does he or she vary tone of voice?
- Does the student vary voice when reading dialogue?

Student's Comments: This portion of the chart is important to complete because it encourages self-evaluation. After the student reads the passage, ask him or her the questions below and record pertinent responses.

- How do you feel about the way you read the passage?
- Was the passage difficult for you?
- Was your reading choppy or smooth?
- Did you read slowly or at a quick pace?
- Did you make many mistakes?
- How do you feel about your use of expression?

Student Name _____

Parent Name _____

Fluency Chart

Passage: _____

Smooth Reading: _____

_____

_____

_____

Reading Rates: _____

_____

_____

_____

Accuracy: _____

_____

_____

_____

Expression: _____

_____

_____

_____

Student's Comments: _____

_____

_____

_____

_____

Waiting for the Pony Express

Objective

√ Students will participate in cooperative learning and improve expressive reading skills by engaging in reader's theater.

Preparation

- Copy *The Pony Express from* Roughing It (page 34) for the teacher.
- Copy *The Pony Express Reader's Theater* (pages 35–38) for each student.
- Provide highlighters.

Fluency Suggestions and Activities

You may want to complete the history and vocabulary activities on the following page before starting this fluency activity. An understanding of the historical context and vocabulary will help students analyze and read the piece fluently.

Note: You might want to have students complete this activity on January 8, Postal Day, in honor of the United States postal workers in your community.

1. Model a fluent reading of *The Pony Express from* Roughing It (page 34) for the students. Tell students that they will be performing this for a group of United States postal workers in their community.

2. Give each student a copy of *The Pony Express Reader's Theater* (pages 35–38). There are 10 parts in this reader's theater. Assign parts to students by having them volunteer or audition. Have students highlight their parts. If you have more then 10 students, divide the parts to allow the entire class to participate in the reading. Or, have multiple readings of the piece.

3. Read the script with the students. Model reading lines with changes in pitch, tone, and timing to achieve different effects. Ask students to look for clues in the text that tell them how to read it (e.g., commas or exclamation points).

4. Students should then begin to practice reading their assigned parts aloud.

5. Once the students are comfortable, have them perform their readings for some postal workers in your community. Arrange ahead of time for some workers from the local post office to come to your class to hear the reader's theater.

Waiting for the Pony Express (cont.)

History Connection

Introduce the Pony Express using the information provided below.

The Pony Express ran from April 1860 to November 1861. It began as a way to deliver mail between St. Joseph, Missouri, and Sacramento, California. About 180 riders traveled this route and earned about $100 a month. They traveled day and night and all year around. Each of them had to weigh less than 125 pounds and they ranged in age from 11 to 45. Their horses were exchanged every 10 to 15 miles and the riders changed every 75 to 100 miles. This route improved communication between the East and the West and kept those in California informed about the beginning of the Civil War.

Vocabulary Connection

Discuss unfamiliar vocabulary encountered in the text. Some possible words are listed below. After identifying the difficult words, discuss them within the context of the text.

- **perishable**—something that can die
- **crags and precipices**—rough cliffs
- **utmost**—highest or best
- **steed**—horse
- **spectator**—those watching the action
- **pantaloons**—pant legs
- **frivolous**—unimportant
- **primer**—beginning reading book
- **economized**—saved
- **procession**—parade or line of people
- **gallant**—brave
- **phantom**—ghost
- **belated**—late

Extension Idea

- Have students trace the trail of the Pony Express riders on a map. Then, they can research additional facts about the Pony Express riders and create game cards with questions and answers to entertain the postal workers on their visit.

The Pony Express from Roughing It

By Mark Twain

In a little while all interest was taken up in stretching our necks and watching for the "pony-rider"—the fleet messenger who sped across the continent from St. Joe to Sacramento, carrying letters nineteen hundred miles in eight days! Think of that for perishable horse and human flesh and blood to do! The pony-rider was usually a little bit of a man, brimful of spirit and endurance. No matter what time of the day or night his watch came on, and no matter whether it was winter or summer, raining, snowing, hailing, or sleeting, or whether his "beat" was a level straight road or a crazy trail over mountain crags and precipices, or whether it led through peaceful regions or regions that swarmed with hostile Indians, he must be always ready to leap into the saddle and be off like the wind! There was no idling-time for a pony-rider on duty. He rode fifty miles without stopping, by daylight, moonlight, starlight, or through the blackness of darkness—just as it happened. He rode a splendid horse that was born for a racer and fed and lodged like a gentleman; kept him at his utmost speed for ten miles, and then, as he came crashing up to the station where stood two men holding fast a fresh, impatient steed, the transfer of rider and mail-bag was made in the twinkling of an eye, and away flew the eager pair and were out of sight before the spectator could get hardly the ghost of a look. Both rider and horse went "flying light." The rider's dress was thin, and fitted close; he wore a "round-about," and a skull-cap, and tucked his pantaloons into his boot-tops like a race-rider. He carried no arms—he carried nothing that was not absolutely necessary, for even the postage on his literary freight was worth *five dollars a letter.*

He got but little frivolous correspondence to carry—his bag had business letters in it, mostly. His horse was stripped of all unnecessary weight, too. He wore a little wafer of a racing-saddle, and no visible blanket. He wore light shoes, or none at all. The little flat mail-pockets strapped under the rider's thighs would each hold about the bulk of a child's primer. They held many and many an important business chapter and newspaper letter, but these were written on paper as airy and thin as gold-leaf, nearly, and thus bulk and weight were economized. The stage-coach traveled about a hundred to a hundred and twenty-five miles a day (twenty-four hours), the pony-rider about two hundred and fifty. There were about eighty pony-riders in the saddle all the time, night and day, stretching in a long, scattering procession from Missouri to California, forty flying eastward, and forty toward the west, and among them making four hundred gallant horses earn a stirring livelihood and see a deal of scenery every single day in the year.

We had had a consuming desire, from the beginning, to see a pony-rider, but somehow or other all that passed us and all that met us managed to streak by in the night, and so we heard only a whiz and a hail, and the swift phantom of the desert was gone before we could get our heads out of the windows. But now we were expecting one along every moment, and would see him in broad daylight. Presently the driver exclaims:

"HERE HE COMES!"

Every neck is stretched further, and every eye strained wider. Away across the endless dead level of the prairie a black speck appears against the sky, and it is plain that it moves. Well, I should think so!

In a second or two it becomes a horse and rider, rising and falling, rising and falling—sweeping toward us nearer and nearer—growing more and more distinct, more and more sharply defined—nearer and still nearer, and the flutter of the hoofs comes faintly to the ear—another instant a whoop and a hurrah from our upper deck, a wave of the rider's hand, but no reply, and man and horse burst past our excited faces, and go winging away like a belated fragment of a storm!

So sudden is it all, and so like a flash of unreal fancy, that but for the flake of white foam left quivering and perishing on a mail-sack after the vision had flashed by and disappeared, we might have doubted whether we had seen any actual horse and man at all, maybe.

Name _____

The Pony Express Reader's Theater

R1: In a little while all interest was taken up in stretching our necks and watching for the "pony-rider"

R2: the fleet messenger who sped across the continent from St. Joe to Sacramento,

R3: carrying letters 1,900 miles in eight days!

All: **Think of that for perishable horse and human flesh and blood to do!**

R4: The pony-rider was usually a little bit of a man, brimful of spirit and endurance.

R5: No matter what time of the day or night his watch came on,

R6: and no matter whether it was winter or summer, raining, snowing, hailing, or sleeting, or whether his "beat" was a level straight road or a crazy trail over mountain crags and precipices,

R7: or whether it led through peaceful regions or regions that swarmed with hostile Indians,

All: **he must be always ready to leap into the saddle and be off like the wind!**

R8: There was no idling-time for a pony-rider on duty.

R9: He rode 50 miles without stopping, by daylight, moonlight, starlight, or through the blackness of darkness—just as it happened.

R10: He rode a splendid horse that was born for a racer and fed and lodged like a gentleman; kept him at his utmost speed for 10 miles,

R1: and then, as he came crashing up to the station where stood two men holding fast a fresh, impatient steed, the transfer of rider and mail-bag was made in the twinkling of an eye,

The Pony Express Reader's Theater (cont.)

R2: and away flew the eager pair and were out of sight before the spectator could get hardly the ghost of a look.

All: Both rider and horse went "flying light."

R3: The rider's dress was thin, and fitted close;

R4: he wore a "round-about,"

R5: and a skull-cap,

R6: and tucked his pantaloons into his boot-tops like a race-rider.

All: He carried no arms—

R7: he carried nothing that was not absolutely necessary,

R8: for even the postage on his literary freight was worth *five dollars a letter.*

R9: He got but little frivolous correspondence to carry—

R10: his bag had business letters in it, mostly.

All: His horse was stripped of all unnecessary weight, too.

R1: He wore a little wafer of a racing-saddle, and no visible blanket.

R2: He wore light shoes,

R3: or none at all.

R4: The little flat mail-pockets strapped under the rider's thighs would each hold about the bulk of a child's primer.

R5: They held many and many an important business chapter and newspaper letter, but these were written on paper as airy and thin as gold-leaf, nearly, and thus bulk and weight were economized.

The Pony Express Reader's Theater *(cont.)*

All: The stage-coach traveled about a 100 to a 125 miles a day (24 hours), the pony-rider about 250.

R6: There were about 80 pony-riders in the saddle all the time, night and day, stretching in a long, scattering procession from Missouri to California,

R7: 40 flying eastward,

R8: and 40 toward the west,

R9: and among them making 400 gallant horses earn a stirring livelihood and see a deal of scenery every single day in the year.

R10: We had had a consuming desire, from the beginning, to see a pony-rider, but somehow or other all that passed us and all that met us managed to streak by in the night,

R1: and so we heard only a whiz and a hail, and the swift phantom of the desert was gone before we could get our heads out of the windows.

R2: But now we were expecting one along every moment, and would see him in broad daylight. Presently the driver exclaims:

All: "HERE HE COMES!"

R3: Every neck is stretched further, and every eye strained wider.

R4: Away across the endless dead level of the prairie a black speck appears against the sky, and it is plain that it moves. Well, I should think so!

R5: In a second or two it becomes a horse and rider,

R6: rising and falling, rising and falling—

The Pony Express Reader's Theater (cont.)

R7:   sweeping toward us nearer and nearer—

R8:   growing more and more distinct, more and more sharply defined—

R9:   nearer and still nearer,

R10: and the flutter of the hoofs comes faintly to the ear—

R1:   another instant a whoop and a hurrah from our upper deck,

R2:   a wave of the rider's hand, but no reply,

R3:   and man and horse burst past our excited faces,

R4:   and go winging away like a belated fragment of a storm!

R5:   So sudden is it all,

R6:   and so like a flash of unreal fancy,

R7:   that but for the flake of white foam

R8:   left quivering

R9:   and perishing on a mail-sack

R10: after the vision had flashed by and disappeared,

All: **we might have doubted whether we had seen any actual horse and man at all, maybe.**

The Trip West

Objective

√ Students will read "Sweet Betsy from Pike" using call-and-response method.

Preparation

- Make a transparency of the song, "Sweet Betsy from Pike" (page 41).
- Copy *"Sweet Betsy from Pike"—Call and Response* (pages 42–43) for each student.
- For optional use, copy *Planning a Trip for Betsy and Ike* (page 44) for each student.
- Gather some maps showing the pioneer trails, including the California Trail.

Fluency Suggestions and Activities

You may want to complete the history and vocabulary activities on the following page before starting this fluency activity. An understanding of the historical context and vocabulary will help students analyze and read the piece fluently.

Note: You might want to complete this activity toward the end of the school year as a celebration of the students passing into a new grade level, their new frontier.

1. Begin by asking students what they know about pioneer life. Have students brainstorm their ideas on the board. Then, place the transparency of the song, "Sweet Betsy from Pike" (page 41), on the overhead and read it aloud, modeling fluent reading for the students. This song has many versions. The stanzas included here are those that are the most relevant to the unit of study.

2. Provide maps of the pioneer trails for students to see the route that Ike and Betsy traveled in this song (the California Trail).

3. Give each student a copy of *"Sweet Betsy from Pike"—Call and Response* (pages 42–43) and read it aloud together several times. Model reading lines with changes in pitch, tone, and timing to achieve different effects. Although this is a song, you are treating it like a poem.

4. Tell students that they will work in groups to perform a reading of this song for the music teacher(s) in your school. Divide students into nine groups. Each group will be responsible for reading a section of the song. The entire class will read the chorus together. Allow time for the students to practice the song several times.

5. When each group feels comfortable, have the class perform a reading of this song for their guest(s).

The Trip West (cont.)

History Connection

Introduce "Sweet Betsy from Pike" using the information provided below.

For most nineteenth century pioneers, making the trip to the West was very difficult. They recorded their hardships in journals and diaries. Songs were written from these journals. This song was written in 1847, as the pioneers were traveling to California for the gold rush. It tells a story about a man named Ike and a woman named Betsy who traveled the California Trail in the 1840s and experienced hardships along the way. They begin in Pike County, Illinois. In the full text of the song, Indians attack them, their animals died or ran off, their wagon was wrecked, and their food ran out.

Vocabulary Connection

Discuss unfamiliar vocabulary encountered in the text. Some possible words are listed below. After identifying the difficult words, discuss them within the context of the text.

- **Platte**—a river along the Oregon and California trails
- **repose**—rest or sleep
- **Placerville**—a city in northern California toward the end of the California trail
- **Hangtown**—another name for Placerville

Extension Ideas

- Have students write another verse to go with this song. Does it fit with the story? Does the verse address a hardship that pioneers faced? Have students vote on the new verses and allow them to add the winning verse to their performance.
- Have students act as travel agents for Betsy and Ike. Distribute copies of *Planning a Trip for Betsy and Ike* (page 44). Students will need access to atlas maps or the Internet.

Sweet Betsy from Pike

Oh don't you remember sweet Betsy from Pike,
Who crossed the wide prairie with her lover Ike,
With two yoke of oxen, a big yellow dog,
A tall shanghai rooster, and one spotted hog?

Chorus:
Singing too-ral-li-oo-ral-li-oo-ral-li-ay,
Singing too-ral-li-oo-ral-li-oo-ral-li-ay.

One evening quite early they camped on the Platte.
'Twas near by the road on a green shady flat.
Where Betsy, sore-footed, lay down to repose—
With wonder Ike gazed on that Pike County rose.

The Indians came down in a wild yelling horde,
And Betsy was scared they would scalp her adored;
Behind the front wagon wheel Betsy did crawl,
And there fought the Injuns with musket and ball.

They soon reached the desert where Betsy gave out,
And down in the sand she lay rolling about;
While Ike, half distracted, looked on with surprise,
Saying, "Betsy, get up, you'll get sand in your eyes."

Sweet Betsy got up in a great deal of pain,
Declared she'd go back to Pike County again;
But Ike gave a sigh and they fondly embraced,
And they traveled along with his arm round her waist.

The shanghai ran off, and their cattle all died;
That morning the last piece of bacon was fried;
Poor Ike was discouraged and Betsy got mad,
The dog drooped his tail and looked wondrously sad.

The terrible desert was burning and bare,
And Isaac he shrank from the death lurkin' there,
"Dear old Pike County, I'll come back to you."
Says Betsy, "You'll go by yourself if you do."

They suddenly stopped on a very high hill,
With wonder looked down upon old Placerville;
Ike sighed when he said, and he cast his eyes down,
"Sweet Betsy, my darling, we've got to Hangtown."

They swam wild rivers and climbed the tall peaks,
And camped on the prairies for weeks upon weeks,
Starvation and cholera, hard work and slaughter,
They reached Californy, spite of hell and high water.

Name _____

"Sweet Betsy from Pike"— Call and Response

G1:   Oh don't you remember sweet Betsy from Pike,
Who crossed the wide prairie with her lover Ike,
With two yoke of oxen, a big yellow dog,
A tall shanghai rooster, and one spotted hog?

All: **Singing too-ral-li-oo-ral-li-oo-ral-li-ay,**
Singing too-ral-li-oo-ral-li-oo-ral-li-ay.

G2:   One evening quite early they camped on the Platte.
'Twas near by the road on a green shady flat.
Where Betsy, sore-footed, lay down to repose—
With wonder Ike gazed on that Pike County rose.

All: **Singing too-ral-li-oo-ral-li-oo-ral-li-ay,**
Singing too-ral-li-oo-ral-li-oo-ral-li-ay.

G3:   The Indians came down in a wild yelling horde,
And Betsy was scared they would scalp her adored;
Behind the front wagon wheel Betsy did crawl,
And there fought the Injuns with musket and ball.

All: **Singing too-ral-li-oo-ral-li-oo-ral-li-ay,**
Singing too-ral-li-oo-ral-li-oo-ral-li-ay.

G4:   They soon reached the desert where Betsy gave out,
And down in the sand she lay rolling about;
While Ike, half distracted, looked on with surprise,
Saying, "Betsy, get up, you'll get sand in your eyes."

All: **Singing too-ral-li-oo-ral-li-oo-ral-li-ay,**
Singing too-ral-li-oo-ral-li-oo-ral-li-ay.

G5:   Sweet Betsy got up in a great deal of pain,
Declared she'd go back to Pike County again;
But Ike gave a sigh and they fondly embraced,
And they traveled along with his arm round her waist.

All: **Singing too-ral-li-oo-ral-li-oo-ral-li-ay,**
Singing too-ral-li-oo-ral-li-oo-ral-li-ay.

Name _____

"Sweet Betsy from Pike"— Call and Response

G6:　The shanghai ran off, and their cattle all died;
　　　That morning the last piece of bacon was fried;
　　　Poor Ike was discouraged and Betsy got mad,
　　　The dog drooped his tail and looked wondrously sad.

All:　**Singing too-ral-li-oo-ral-li-oo-ral-li-ay,**
　　　Singing too-ral-li-oo-ral-li-oo-ral-li-ay.

G7:　The terrible desert was burning and bare,
　　　And Isaac he shrank from the death lurkin' there,
　　　"Dear old Pike County, I'll come back to you."
　　　Says Betsy, "You'll go by yourself if you do."

All:　**Singing too-ral-li-oo-ral-li-oo-ral-li-ay,**
　　　Singing too-ral-li-oo-ral-li-oo-ral-li-ay.

G8:　They suddenly stopped on a very high hill,
　　　With wonder looked down upon old Placerville;
　　　Ike sighed when he said, and he cast his eyes down,
　　　"Sweet Betsy, my darling, we've got to Hangtown."

All:　**Singing too-ral-li-oo-ral-li-oo-ral-li-ay,**
　　　Singing too-ral-li-oo-ral-li-oo-ral-li-ay.

G9:　They swam wild rivers and climbed the tall peaks,
　　　And camped on the prairies for weeks upon weeks,
　　　Starvation and cholera, hard work and slaughter,
　　　They reached Californy, spite of hell and high water.

All:　**Singing too-ral-li-oo-ral-li-oo-ral-li-ay,**
　　　Singing too-ral-li-oo-ral-li-oo-ral-li-ay.

Name _____

Planning a Trip for Betsy and Ike

Directions: You are the travel agent in charge of planning Betsy and Ike's trip to California. They have hired you to choose the best trail and to tell them about the accommodations along the way. Plan their trip below.

1. Betsy and Ike need a map showing the route you have chosen. Choose a different route than the one they traveled, the California Trail. How is your route better for them?

2. Use a mapping program from the Internet or a copy of a printed map from an atlas to map out their way. Trace the best route for them.

3. Suppose Betsy and Ike refuse your advice on a trail. They choose the trail from Pike County, Illinois, to Placerville, California. Look at a map. How many miles is this route? How many miles is the route that you proposed?

4. Wagon trains traveled two miles per hour. How many hours would it take them to get there using your route? How many hours would it take using their route?

5. What things should Betsy and Ike be aware of when traveling your route? Create a top 10 "be aware of" list for them. Add a creative solution for every danger they might encounter.

1. _____

2. _____

3. _____

4. _____

5. _____

6. _____

7. _____

8. _____

9. _____

10. _____

The Lady Who Started a War

Objective

√ Students will participate in cooperative learning and improve expressive reading skills by engaging in reader's theater.

Preparation

- Copy *Uncle Tom's Cabin—Reader's Theater* (pages 49–52) for each student.
- Provide highlighters.

Fluency Suggestions and Activities

You may want to complete the history and vocabulary activities on the following page before starting this fluency activity. An understanding of the historical context and vocabulary will help students analyze and read the piece fluently.

Note: You might want to plan to complete this fluency activity during Black History Month or during a unit on slavery.

1. Explain to the students that they will read the text for this lesson in the form of reader's theater. Review with the students that reader's theater is a shared-reading activity, where several students take turns reading parts of the text. Some parts of the selection are read by individual students, and some parts are read by all students.

2. Divide the students into groups of five and distribute copies of *Uncle Tom's Cabin— Reader's Theater* (pages 49–52). The original text from *Uncle Tom's Cabin* has been provided on pages 47–48 for your reference. For the reader's theater, the language of the time period has been edited slightly to help students read the text more fluently.

3. Assign each student in the group a part to read and have the students highlight their parts. Parts are labeled R1 (for Reader 1) to R5. Draw their attention to the parts to be read by "All" students. These are emphasized in bold print. Have the students discuss words or phrases that should carry particular expressive emphasis. Allow students time in class to practice their readings of the text.

4. For the actual performance, divide the whole text into shorter parts so that each group will have a chance to participate. Allow plenty of time for students to practice the reading in this way before the performance.

5. Explain to students that they will be performing this reader's theater for a "special session of Congress" that will include various school officials. Have students create invitations for these school officials and arrange for them to be present at the performance.

6. Explain that the audience (the Congress) will need to have more background information about *Uncle Tom's Cabin* and the Fugitive Slave Act. To do this, students will need to create an introduction to their reader's theater. The introduction can be a short paragraph read by one student or it can be presented in reader's theater format.

The Lady Who Started a War *(cont.)*

History Connection

Introduce *Uncle Tom's Cabin* using the information provided below.

After putting her children to bed at night, Harriet Beecher Stowe sat down in her kitchen and wrote about slavery. She was appalled by the Fugitive Slave Act of 1850, which punished citizens who helped slaves run away. She had never personally seen slaves in the Deep South, but she had witnessed slavery in Kentucky. In 1852, she published her book called *Uncle Tom's Cabin*. It told a story about a black slave who was mistreated by his white owner. Stowe's book became a popular piece of antislavery writing and caused quite a bit of tension between the North and the South.

Vocabulary Connection

Discuss unfamiliar vocabulary encountered in the text. Some possible words are listed below. After identifying the difficult words, discuss them within the context of the text.

- **rheumatism**—a disease that inflames the joints
- **trepidation**—a fearful feeling
- **evolutions**—turns around
- **agility**—smooth movement
- **contemptuous**—expressing dislike or lack of respect
- **auctioneer**—person who controls the bidding at an auction
- **vehemently**—with strong feeling, forcefully
- **stentorian**—loud and powerful
- **commence**—begin
- **simultaneously**—at the same time
- **contending**—competing
- **kink**—imperfection
- **destitute**—lacking
- **disperse**—leave

Extension Idea

- Have students create a book jacket for *Uncle Tom's Cabin*. They can include quotes from famous people recommending the book, a summary of the book, a short interview with Stowe on why she wrote the book, and any awards or best seller lists that the book achieved.

Uncle Tom's Cabin— Excerpt from Chapter 12

By Harriet Beecher Stowe

The men and women to be sold sat in a group apart, talking in a low tone to each other. The woman who had been advertised by the name of Hagar was a regular African in feature and figure. She might have been sixty, but was older than that by hard work and disease, was partially blind, and somewhat crippled with rheumatism. By her side stood her only remaining son, Albert, a bright-looking little fellow of fourteen years. The boy was the only survivor of a large family, who had been successively sold away from her to a southern market. The mother held on to him with both her shaking hands, and eyed with intense trepidation every one who walked up to examine him.

"Don't be feard, Aunt Hagar," said the oldest of the men, "I spoke to Mas'r Thomas 'bout it, and he thought he might manage to sell you in a lot both together."

"Dey needn't call me worn out yet," said she, lifting her shaking hands. "I can cook yet, and scrub, and scour,—I'm wuth a buying, if I do come cheap;—tell em dat ar,—you *tell* em," she added, earnestly.

Haley here forced his way into the group, walked up to the old man, pulled his mouth open and looked in, felt of his teeth, made him stand and straighten himself, bend his back, and perform various evolutions to show his muscles; and then passed on to the next, and put him through the same trial. Walking up last to the boy, he felt of his arms, straightened his hands, and looked at his fingers, and made him jump, to show his agility.

"He an't gwine to be sold widout me!" said the old woman, with passionate eagerness; "He and I goes in a lot together; I's rail strong yet, Mas'r and can do heaps o' work,—heaps on it, Mas'r."

"On plantation?" said Haley, with a contemptuous glance. "Likely story!" and, as if satisfied with his examination, he walked out and looked, and stood with his hands in his pocket, his cigar in his mouth, and his hat cocked on one side, ready for action.

"What think of 'em?" said a man who had been following Haley's examination, as if to make up his own mind from it.

"Wal," said Haley, spitting, "I shall put in, I think, for the youngerly ones and the boy."

"They want to sell the boy and the old woman together," said the man.

"Find it a tight pull;—why, she's an old rack o' bones,—not worth her salt."

"You wouldn't then?" said the man.

"Anybody 'd be a fool 't would. She's half blind, crooked with rheumatis, and foolish to boot."

"Some buys up these yer old crittus, and ses there's a sight more wear in 'em than a body 'd think," said the man, reflectively.

"No go, 't all," said Haley; "wouldn't take her for a present,—fact,—I've *seen*, now."

"Wal, 't is kinder pity, now, not to buy her with her son,—her heart seems so sot on him,— s'pose they fling her in cheap."

"Them that's got money to spend that ar way, it's all well enough. I shall bid off on that ar boy for a plantation-hand;—wouldn't be bothered with her, no way, notif they'd give her to me," said Haley.

Uncle Tom's Cabin— Excerpt from Chapter 12 *(cont.)*

"She'll take on desp't," said the man.

"Nat'lly, she will," said the trader, coolly.

The conversation was here interrupted by a busy hum in the audience; and the auctioneer, a short, bustling, important fellow, elbowed his way into the crowd. The old woman drew in her breath, and caught instinctively at her son.

"Keep close to yer mammy, Albert,—close,—dey'll put us up togedder," she said.

"O, mammy, I'm fear'd they won't," said the boy.

"Dey must, child; I can't live, no ways, if they don't" said the old creature, vehemently.

The stentorian tones of the auctioneer, calling out to clear the way, now announced that the sale was about to commence. A place was cleared, and the bidding began. The different men on the list were soon knocked off at prices which showed a pretty brisk demand in the market; two of them fell to Haley.

"Come, now, young un," said the auctioneer, giving the boy a touch with his hammer, "be up and show your springs, now."

"Put us two up togedder, togedder,—do please, Mas'r," said the old woman, holding fast to her boy.

"Be off," said the man, gruffly, pushing her hands away; "you come last. Now, darkey, spring;" and, with the word, he pushed the boy toward the block, while a deep, heavy groan rose behind him. The boy paused, and looked back; but there was no time to stay, and, dashing the tears from his large, bright eyes, he was up in a moment.

His fine figure, alert limbs, and bright face, raised an instant competition, and half a dozen bids simultaneously met the ear of the auctioneer. Anxious, half-frightened, he looked from side to side, as he heard the clatter of contending bids,—now here, now there,—till the hammer fell. Haley had got him. He was pushed from the block toward his new master, but stopped one moment, and looked back, when his poor old mother, trembling in every limb, held out her shaking hands toward him.

"Buy me too, Mas'r, for de dear Lord's sake!—buy me,—I shall die if you don't!"

"You'll die if I do, that's the kink of it," said Haley,—"no!" And he turned on his heel.

The bidding for the poor old creature was summary. The man who had addressed Haley, and who seemed not destitute of compassion, bought her for a trifle, and the spectators began to disperse.

The poor victims of the sale, who had been brought up in one place together for years, gathered round the despairing old mother, whose agony was pitiful to see.

"Couldn't dey leave me one? Mas'r allers said I should have one,—he did," she repeated over and over, in heart-broken tones.

"Trust in the Lord, Aunt Hagar," said the oldest of the men, sorrowfully.

"What good will it do?" said she, sobbing passionately.

Name _____

Uncle Tom's Cabin—Reader's Theater

R1: The men and women to be sold sat in a group apart, talking in a low tone to each other.

R2: The woman who had been advertised by the name of Hagar was a regular African in feature and figure.

R3: She might have been 60, but was older than that by hard work and disease, was partially blind, and somewhat crippled with rheumatism.

R4: By her side stood her only remaining son, Albert, a bright-looking little fellow of 14 years. The boy was the only survivor of a large family, who had been successively sold away from her to a southern market.

R5: The mother held on to him with both her shaking hands, and eyed with intense trepidation every one who walked up to examine him.

R1: "Don't be feared, Aunt Hagar," said the oldest of the men, "I spoke to Mas'r Thomas about it, and he thought he might manage to sell you in a lot both together."

All: **"They needn't call me worn out yet," said she, lifting her shaking hands.**

R2: "I can cook yet, and scrub, and scour,—I'm worth buying, if I do come cheap;—tell em that there,—you tell em," she added, earnestly.

R3: Haley forced his way into the group, walked up to the old man,

R4: pulled his mouth open and looked in, felt of his teeth, made him stand and straighten himself,

R5: bend his back, and perform various evolutions to show his muscles;

R1: and then passed on to the next,

R2: and put him through the same trial.

Uncle Tom's Cabin—Reader's Theater (cont.)

R3: Walking up last to the boy, he felt of his arms, straightened his hands,

R4: and looked at his fingers, and made him jump, to show his agility.

All: **"He ain't going to be sold without me!" said the old woman, with passionate eagerness;**

R5: "He and I goes in a lot together; I is real strong yet, Mas'r and can do heaps o' work,—heaps on it, Mas'r."

R1: "On plantation?" said Haley, with a contemptuous glance. "Likely story!"

R2: and, as if satisfied with his examination, he walked out and looked, and stood with his hands in his pocket, his cigar in his mouth, and his hat cocked on one side, ready for action.

R3: "What think of 'em?" said a man who had been following Haley's examination, as if to make up his own mind from it.

R4: "Well," said Haley, spitting, "I shall put in, I think, for the youngerly ones and the boy."

R5: "They want to sell the boy and the old woman together," said the man.

R1: "Find it a tight pull;—why, she's an old rack o' bones,—not worth her salt."

R2: "You wouldn't then?" said the man.

R3: "Anybody would be a fool that would. She's half blind, crooked with rheumatis, and foolish to boot."

R4: "Some buys up these here old critturs, and sees there's a sight more wear in 'em than a body would think," said the man, reflectively.

R5: "No go, at all," said Haley; "wouldn't take her for a present,—fact,—I've seen, now."

R1: "Well, that is kind of a pity, now, not to buy her with her son,—her heart seems so sot on him,—suppose they fling her in cheap."

Uncle Tom's Cabin—Reader's Theater *(cont.)*

R2: "Them that's got money to spend that there way, it's all well enough. I shall bid off on that there boy for a plantation-hand;—wouldn't be bothered with her, no way, not if they'd give her to me," said Haley.

R3: "She'll take on desperate," said the man.

R4: "Naturally, she will," said the trader, coolly.

R5: The conversation was here interrupted by a busy hum in the audience; and the auctioneer, a short, bustling, important fellow, elbowed his way into the crowd. The old woman drew in her breath, and caught instinctively at her son.

All: **"Keep close to yer mammy, Albert,—close,—they'll put us up together," she said.**

R1: "O, mammy, I'm feared they won't," said the boy.

All: "They must, child; I can't live, no ways, if they don't" said the old creature, vehemently.

R2: The stentorian tones of the auctioneer, calling out to clear the way, now announced that the sale was about to commence.

R3: A place was cleared, and the bidding began.

R4: The different men on the list were soon knocked off at prices which showed a pretty brisk demand in the market; two of them fell to Haley.

R5: "Come, now, young un," said the auctioneer, giving the boy a touch with his hammer, "be up and show your springs, now."

All: **"Put us two up together, together,—do please, Mas'r," said the old woman, holding fast to her boy.**

R1: "Be off," said the man, gruffly, pushing her hands away; "you come last."

R2: and, with the word, he pushed the boy toward the block, while a deep, heavy groan rose behind him.

Uncle Tom's Cabin—Reader's Theater *(cont.)*

R3: The boy paused, and looked back; but there was no time to stay, and, dashing the tears from his large, bright eyes, he was up in a moment.

R4: His fine figure, alert limbs, and bright face, raised an instant competition, and half a dozen bids simultaneously met the ear of the auctioneer.

R5: Anxious, half-frightened, he looked from side to side, as he heard the clatter of contending bids,—now here, now there,—till the hammer fell.

R1: Haley had got him.

R2: He was pushed from the block toward his new master, but stopped one moment, and looked back, when his poor old mother, trembling in every limb, held out her shaking hands toward him.

All: **"Buy me too, Mas'r, for the dear Lord's sake!—buy me,—I shall die if you don't!"**

R3: "You'll die if I do, that's the kink of it," said Haley,—

R4: "No!"

R5: And he turned on his heel.

R1: The bidding for the poor old creature was summary.

R2: The man who had addressed Haley, and who seemed not destitute of compassion, bought her for a trifle,

R3: and the spectators began to disperse.

R4: The poor victims of the sale, who had been brought up in one place together for years, gathered round the despairing old mother, whose agony was pitiful to see.

All: **"Couldn't they leave me one? Mas'r said I should have one,— he did," she repeated over and over, in heart-broken tones.**

R5: "Trust in the Lord, Aunt Hagar," said the oldest of the men, sorrowfully.

All: **"What good will it do?" said she, sobbing passionately.**

Letting the Slaves Go

Objective

√ Students will read "Go Down Moses" using call-and-response method.

Preparation

- Make an overhead transparency of the song, "Go Down, Moses" (page 55).
- Copy *"Go Down, Moses"—Call and Response* (pages 56–58) for each student.
- For optional use, copy *Announcing Emancipation* (page 58) for each student.

Fluency Suggestions and Activities

You may want to complete the history and vocabulary activities on the following page before starting this fluency activity. An understanding of the historical context and vocabulary will help students analyze and read the piece fluently.

Note: You might want to have students complete this reading during Black History Month in February or just before Passover in the spring.

1. Begin by placing the transparency of the song, "Go Down, Moses" (page 55), on the overhead projector and reading it aloud to model fluency.

2. Tell students that they will be performing a reading of this song for some religious leaders in the community. Invite various pastors, priests, rabbis, and rectors from your community to come hear the reading.

3. There are 11 parts in the performance (G1 through G11). Divide students into 11 small groups and distribute copies of *"Go Down, Moses"—Call and Response* (pages 56–57). Tell students that everyone in the class will read the chorus together.

4. Provide time for the groups to practice their parts until everyone is comfortable. Encourage students to include hand motions and facial expressions as they read. Also have the whole class practice together so that groups get used to the flow of the whole piece.

5. On the day of the presentation, have the class perform its call and response. They can choose to involve the audience by distributing a copy of the chorus to their guests. If the audience feels comfortable joining in, they will have the correct words to do so.

Letting the Slaves Go (cont.)

History Connection

Introduce "Go Down, Moses" using the information provided below.

"Go Down Moses" is both a folk song and an African spiritual. Black slaves living in the South created this song. They sung it as they worked, prayed, and rested. It was common for slaves to identify themselves with those in the Bible as they sought to be free from the bondage of slavery. It remains a popular folk song even today.

Vocabulary Connection

Discuss unfamiliar vocabulary encountered in the text. Some possible words are listed below. After identifying the difficult words, discuss them within the context of the text.

- **oppressed**—treated cruelly
- **pharaoh**—leader of the Egyptians
- **smite**—to hit
- **toil**—work
- **spoil**—riches from the land
- **forlorn**—sad or lonely
- **Canaan**—the promised land

Extension Ideas

- Have students find partners for this activity. Each partner will create a drawing from a different perspective. One student will create a drawing of this song using the Hebrews and Egyptians. The other student will create a drawing showing the slaves and their owners. Have each pair of students display their drawings next to each other. Allow students to analyze the ways these two drawings are alike and the ways they are different. Use these pictures as a display for the day of the presentation. Students can provide background information for the audience as they view the pictures. Then, they can present their reading of the song.

- Distribute copies of *Announcing Emancipation* (page 58) to the students. Students will be creating a newspaper article that describes the "local" reaction to the document.

Go Down, Moses

When Israel was in Egypt's land,
Let my people go!
Oppressed so hard they could not stand,
Let my people go!

Chorus:
Go down, Moses,
Way down in Egypt's land.
Tell old Pharaoh
To let my people go!

"Thus spoke the Lord," bold Moses said
"Let my people go!
If not, I'll smite your firstborn dead
Let my people go!"

Repeat Chorus

No more shall they in bondage toil
Let my people go!
Let them come out with Egypt's spoil
Let my people go!

Repeat Chorus

The Lord told Moses what to do
Let my people go!
To lead the Hebrew children through
Let my people go!

Repeat Chorus

O come along Moses, you'll not get lost
Let my people go!
Stretch out your rod and come across.
Let my people go!

Repeat Chorus

As Israel stood by the water side
Let my people go!
At God's command it did divide
Let my people go!

Repeat Chorus

When they reached the other shore
Let my people go!
They sang a song of triumph o'er
Let my people go!

Repeat Chorus

Pharaoh said he'd go across
Let my people go!
But Pharaoh and his host were lost
Let my people go!

Repeat Chorus

O let us all from bondage flee
Let my people go!
And let us all in Christ be free
Let my people go!

Repeat Chorus

You need not always weep and mourn
Let my people go!
And wear these slav'ry chains forlorn
Let my people go!

Repeat Chorus

Your foes shall not before you stand
Let my people go!
And you'll possess fair Canaan's land.
Let my people go!

Repeat Chorus

Name _____

"Go Down, Moses"—Call and Response

G1: When Israel was in Egypt's land,
Let my people go!
Oppressed so hard they could not
   stand,
Let my people go!

All: **Go down, Moses,**
Way down in Egypt's land.
Tell old Pharaoh
To let my people go!

G2: "Thus spoke the Lord," bold Moses
   said
"Let my people go!
If not, I'll smite your firstborn dead
Let my people go!"

All: **Go down, Moses,**
Way down in Egypt's land.
Tell old Pharaoh
To let my people go!

G3: No more shall they in bondage toil
Let my people go!
Let them come out with Egypt's spoil
Let my people go!

All: **Go down, Moses,**
Way down in Egypt's land.
Tell old Pharaoh
To let my people go!

G4: The Lord told Moses what to do
Let my people go!
To lead the Hebrew children through
Let my people go!

All: **Go down, Moses,**
Way down in Egypt's land.
Tell old Pharaoh
To let my people go!

G5: O come along Moses, you'll not
   get lost
Let my people go!
Stretch out your rod and come
   across.
Let my people go!

All: **Go down, Moses,**
Way down in Egypt's land.
Tell old Pharaoh
To let my people go!

G6: As Israel stood by the water side
Let my people go!
At God's command it did divide
Let my people go!

All: **Go down, Moses,**
Way down in Egypt's land.
Tell old Pharaoh
To let my people go!

G7: When they reached the other
   shore
Let my people go!
They sang a song of triumph o'er
Let my people go!

All: **Go down, Moses,**
Way down in Egypt's land.
Tell old Pharaoh
To let my people go!

G8: Pharaoh said he'd go across
Let my people go!
But Pharaoh and his host were
   lost
Let my people go!

"Go Down, Moses"— Call and Response (cont.)

All: **Go down, Moses,**
Way down in Egypt's land.
Tell old Pharaoh
To let my people go

G9:   O let us all from bondage flee
Let my people go!
And let us all in Christ be free
Let my people go!

All: **Go down, Moses,**
Way down in Egypt's land.
Tell old Pharaoh
To let my people go!

G10:   You need not always weep and mourn
Let my people go!
And wear these slav'ry chains forlorn
Let my people go!

All: **Go down, Moses,**
Way down in Egypt's land.
Tell old Pharaoh
To let my people go!

G11:   Your foes shall not before you stand
Let my people go!
And you'll possess fair Canaan's land.
Let my people go!

All: **Go down, Moses,**
Way down in Egypt's land.
Tell old Pharaoh
To let my people go!

Name _____

Announcing Emancipation

Excerpt from the Emancipation Proclamation

Whereas, on the twenty-second day of September, in the year of our Lord one thousand eight hundred and sixty-two, a proclamation was issued by the President of the United States, containing, among other things, the following, to wit: "That on the first day of January, in the year of our Lord one thousand eight hundred and sixty-three, all persons held as slaves within any State or designated part of a State, the people whereof shall then be in rebellion against the United States, shall be then, thenceforward, and forever free; and the Executive Government of the United States, including the military and naval authority thereof, will recognize and maintain the freedom of such persons, and will do no act or acts to repress such persons, or any of them, in any efforts they may make for their actual freedom."

Directions: A section of the Emancipation Proclamation is written above. This document did not free slaves in the Border States. It applied only to those states in the Confederacy. You are a newspaper reporter from a Southern state or one of the Border States. On another sheet of paper, write a newspaper article announcing the Emancipation Proclamation. Provide a title for your article, important facts about the Emancipation Proclamation, and the local reaction to this document. Be sure to tell if you are from a Southern state or a Border State.

Surrendering at Last

Objective

√ Students will read aloud fluently and accurately with changes in tone, voice, timing, and expression using the strategy of choral reading.

Preparation

- Make an overhead transparency of *I Will Fight No More Forever* (page 61).
- Copy *I Will Fight No More Forever—Choral Reading* (page 62) for each student.
- For optional use, copy *Critiquing Chief Joseph's Speech* (page 63) for each student.

Fluency Suggestions and Activities

You may want to complete the history and vocabulary activities on the following page before starting this fluency activity. An understanding of the historical context and vocabulary will help students analyze and read the piece fluently.

Note: You may want to hold this presentation sometime during the month of November since it has been declared National American Indian Heritage Month.

1. Place a transparency copy of *I Will Fight No More Forever* (page 61) on the overhead projector. Read the speech, modeling fluent reading. Explain to the students that developing fluency isn't just about practicing one's own fluent reading. It also involves listening to other readers.

2. Read the speech with the entire class as a choral reading. Next, have students get into four groups and practice reading the speech chorally with their groups. Then, read the speech a third time with the entire class reading it all together.

3. Distribute *I Will Fight No More Forever—Choral Reading* (page 62). Model how you want students to read the famous speech. Use a great deal of expression and change the volume for dramatic effect. As you progress through the poem, read the repeated line, "I will fight no more forever," differently. You might start in a normal volume, read again a little softer, and then fade to a whisper. After fading to a whisper, gradually increase the volume.

4. Give students ample time to practice reading the speech in their small groups using the style explained above. Finally, practice a full-class reading of the speech.

5. To increase your community's awareness of National American Indian Heritage Month, arrange for students to present a reading of this speech on-air at a local radio station.

Surrendering at Last (cont.)

History Connection

Introduce Chief Joseph's speech using the information provided below.

As the pioneers made their way to the West, the American Indians were forced off their land and placed in reservations. Specifically, the white settlers who traveled the Oregon Trail wanted the lands inhabited by the Nez Percé Indians. So, the government ordered the Nez Percé to go to a reservation in Idaho. Instead of submitting, the Nez Percé refused to leave their land. The U.S. Army tried to make them move, but a fight broke out. The Nez Percé won the first battle, but they knew that the army would not give up. So, they fled towards Canada. As they fled, they fought many small battles with the soldiers along the way. The Indians were finally caught near the Canadian border and their chief, Chief Joseph, had to surrender. This is the famous surrender speech made by Chief Joseph.

Vocabulary Connection

Discuss these two men. These men were killed during the many battles between the Nez Percé and the soldiers. See if students can locate the names of any other Nez Percé who traveled with Chief Joseph.

- **Looking Glass**—a Nez Percé warrior
- **Too-hul-hul-sote**—a Nez Percé warrior

Extension Ideas

- Have students find out where Chief Joseph and his tribe were sent after being captured. Have them plot these places on a map along with the dates that the tribe occupied the sites. They can refer to the map as they prepare to give presentations of their reading.

- Have students critique Chief Joseph's speech as if they were his speech writer. Provide copies of *Critiquing Chief Joseph's Speech* (page 63) to students. They can make changes to this speech and then practice reading it for a friend. After reading their new text a few times, they can ask their friend to compare this new text with the original. Which do they think is a more effective speech?

I Will Fight No More Forever

By Chief Joseph

Tell General Howard I know his heart. What he told me before I have in my heart. I am tired of fighting. Our chiefs are killed. Looking Glass is dead. Too-hul-hul-sote is dead. The old men are all dead. It is the young men who say yes or no. He who led on the young men is dead. It is cold and we have no blankets. The little children are freezing to death. My people, some of them, have run away to the hills, and have no blankets, no food; no one knows where they are—perhaps freezing to death. I want to have time to look for my children and see how many of them I can find. Maybe I shall find them among the dead. Hear me, my chiefs. I am tired; my heart is sick and sad. From where the sun now stands I will fight no more forever.

Name _____

I Will Fight No More Forever— Choral Reading

Tell General Howard I know his heart.

I will fight no more forever

What he told me before I have in my heart. I am tired of fighting.

I will fight no more forever

Our chiefs are killed. Looking Glass is dead.

I will fight no more forever

Too-hul-hul-sote is dead. The old men are all dead.

I will fight no more forever

It is the young men who say yes or no. He who led on the young men is dead.

I will fight no more forever

It is cold and we have no blankets. The little children are freezing to death.

I will fight no more forever

My people, some of them, have run away to the hills, and have no blankets,

I will fight no more forever

no food; no one knows where they are—perhaps freezing to death.

I will fight no more forever

I want to have time to look for my children and see how many of them I can find.

I will fight no more forever

Maybe I shall find them among the dead. Hear me, my chiefs.

I will fight no more forever

I am tired; my heart is sick and sad.

I will fight no more forever

From where the sun now stands

I will fight no more forever.

Name _____

Critiquing Chief Joseph's Speech

Directions: You are the official speechwriter for Chief Joseph. You have been away on a hunting trip and, unfortunately, he wrote this speech without consulting you. What improvements would you make if you had been there to write this speech? Make them in the spaces below.

Tell General Howard I know his heart.

_____

What he told me before I have in my heart. I am tired of fighting.

_____

Our chiefs are killed. Looking Glass is dead.

_____

Too-hul-hul-sote is dead. The old men are all dead.

_____

It is the young men who say yes or no. He who led on the young men is dead.

_____

It is cold and we have no blankets. The little children are freezing to death.

_____

My people, some of them, have run away to the hills, and have no blankets,

_____

no food; no one knows where they are—perhaps freezing to death.

_____

I want to have time to look for my children and see how many of them I can find.

_____

Maybe I shall find them among the dead. Hear me, my chiefs.

_____

I am tired; my heart is sick and sad.

_____

From where the sun now stands

_____

I will fight no more forever.

_____

Red Cloud Speaks

Objective

√ Students will practice oral reading of a divided text in preparation for a videotaped performance.

Preparation

- Copy *Statement on the Causes of Wounded Knee* (page 66) for the teacher.
- Copy *Statement on the Causes of Wounded Knee—Divided Reading* (pages 67–71) for each student.
- Gather a video camera and video tapes.

Fluency Suggestions and Activities

You may want to complete the history and vocabulary activities on the following page before starting this fluency activity. An understanding of the historical context and vocabulary will help students analyze and read the piece fluently.

Note: You might want students to complete this reading around the end of December to remember the massacre on December 29, 1890.

1. Read *Statement on the Causes of Wounded Knee* (page 66) aloud, modeling fluent reading.

2. Divide students into five groups. If possible, show students pictures of Chief Red Cloud. Tell students to imagine that they are Chief Red Cloud. How would they feel giving this speech to the public? What would be their motives for giving the speech? Allow them to discuss their thoughts in their small groups.

3. Assign a section of the story to each group. Distribute copies of *Statement on the Causes of Wounded Knee—Divided Reading* (pages 67–71) to students. You will only need to give each group copies of its own reading excerpt.

4. Tell the class that you will be videotaping their performances of the speech to share with other classes in the school. They might want to think about how they will dress to look like Chief Red Cloud. Have the students in each group read through their sections of the speech.

5. Remind the students to think about how to use their voices to make the speech interesting, with particular expression added to show Chief Red Cloud's emotions. Allow the students several days in class to practice the reading of their sections of the story. Encourage classmates to offer suggestions for improved fluency. The day before the scheduled taping, remind students to bring in props and costumes to add to their presence on the videotape.

6. For the day of the taping, tape each group reading its section of the speech in the correct order so that there will be one entire speech on the tape.

Red Cloud Speaks (cont.)

History Connection

Introduce Red Cloud's speech using the information provided below.

Before being moved to reservations, the Lakota Indians lived in what is today South Dakota, Montana, and Wyoming. Around 1889, many of the Lakota Indians began to believe that an Indian messiah would come to give them back their land that was occupied by the white settlers. They believed that if they performed the Ghost Dance, it would hasten this event. When the government officials saw the Lakota dancing, they became afraid. What was really just a ceremonial dance appeared to be a revolt of some kind. The white people in the area began to fear that the Lakota would try to hurt them. After the death of Chief Sitting Bull, a group of Lakota Indians headed toward a reservation to try to find safety. The U.S. Army captured these Lakota on December 29, 1890, at Wounded Knee Creek. While being disarmed, one Lakota Indian warrior fired his weapon. It took only a few minutes for the soldiers to kill 146 Indians. This speech was made by Red Cloud, the Lakota chief after the massacre. In it, he describes the causes of this terrible event.

Vocabulary Connection

Discuss unfamiliar vocabulary encountered in the text. Some possible words are listed below. After identifying the difficult words, discuss them within the context of the text.

- **treaties**—agreements made between the Indians and the government
- **customs**—traditions
- **means**—supplies and training
- **rations**—predetermined amounts of food to live on for a certain time
- **agitators**—troublemakers
- **slandered**—insulted through words
- **mocked**—made fun of
- **despair**—to give up
- **induced**—convinced

Extension Idea

- Have students work in groups of three students each to create a monument for those American Indians killed at Wounded Knee. Provide students with construction paper, masking tape, packing tape, markers, paintbrushes, and paints. Have each group name its monument and present it to the class during a special ceremony. If possible, place these monuments in the library for display.

Statement on the Causes of Wounded Knee

I will tell you the reason for the trouble. When we first made treaties with the Government, our old life and our old customs were about to end; the game on which we lived was disappearing; the whites were closing around us, and nothing remained for us but to adopt their ways,—the Government promised us all the means necessary to make our living out of the land, and to instruct us how to do it, and with abundant food to support us until we could take care of ourselves. We looked forward with hope to the time we could be as independent as the whites, and have a voice in the Government.

The army officers could have helped better than anyone else but we were not left to them. An Indian Department was made with large number of agents and other officials drawing large salaries—then came the beginning of trouble; these men took care of themselves but not of us. It was very hard to deal with the government through them—they could make more for themselves by keeping us back than by helping us forward.

We did not get the means for working our lands; the few things they gave us did little good.

Our rations began to be reduced; they said we were lazy. That is false. How does any man of sense suppose that so great a number of people could get work at once unless they were at once supplied with the means to work and instructors enough to teach them?

Our ponies were taken away from us under the promise that they would be replaced by oxen and large horses; it was long before we saw any, and then we got very few. We tried with the means we had, but on pretext or another, we were shifted from one place to another, or were told that such a transfer was coming. Great efforts were made to break up our customs, but nothing was done to introduce us to customs of the whites. Everything was done to break up the power of the real chiefs.

Those old men really wished their people to improve, but little men, so-called chiefs, were made to act as disturbers and agitators. Spotted Tail wanted the ways of the whites, but an assassin was found to remove him. This was charged to the Indians because an Indian did it, but who set on the Indian? I was abused and slandered, to weaken my influence for good. This was done by men paid by the government to teach us the ways of the whites. I have visited many other tribes and found that the same things were done amongst them; all was done to discourage us and nothing to encourage us. I saw men paid by the government to help us, all very busy making money for themselves, but doing nothing for us . . .

The men who counted (census) told all around that we were feasting and wasting food. Where did he see it? How could we waste what we did not have? We felt we were mocked in our misery; we had no newspaper and no one to speak for us. Our rations were again reduced.

You who eat three times a day and see your children well and happy around you cannot understand what a starving Indian feels! We were faint with hunger and maddened by despair. We held our dying children and felt their little bodies tremble as their soul went out and left only a dead weight in our hands. They were not very heavy but we were faint and the dead weighed us down. There was no hope on earth. God seemed to have forgotten.

Some one had been talking of the Son of God and said He had come. The people did not know; they did not care; they snatched at hope; they screamed like crazy people to Him for mercy; they caught at the promise they heard He had made.

The white people were frightened and called for soldiers. We begged for life and the white men thought we wanted theirs; we heard the soldiers were coming. We did not fear. We hoped we could tell them our suffering and could get help. The white men told us the soldiers meant to kill us; we did not believe it but some were frightened and ran away to the Bad Lands. The soldiers came. They said: "don't be afraid— we come to make peace, not war." It was true; they brought us food. But the hunger-crazed who had taken fright at the soldiers' coming and went to the Bad Lands could not be induced to return to the horrors of reservation life. They were called Hostiles and the Government sent the army to force them back to their reservation prison.

Name _____

Statement on the Causes of Wounded Knee—Divided Reading

Group 1

I will tell you the reason for the trouble. When we first made treaties with the government, our old life and our old customs were about to end. The animals on which we lived were disappearing. The whites were closing around us, and nothing remained for us but to adopt their ways. The government promised us all the means necessary to make our living out of the land, and to instruct us how to do it, and with abundant food to support us until we could take care of ourselves. We looked forward with hope to the time we could be as independent as the whites, and have a voice in the government.

The army officers could have helped better than anyone else but we were not left to them. An Indian Department was made with large number of agents and other officials drawing large salaries. Then came the beginning of trouble; these men took care of themselves but not of us. It was very hard to deal with the government through them. They could make more for themselves by keeping us back than by helping us forward.

Name _____

Statement on the Causes of Wounded Knee—Divided Reading (cont.)

Group 2

We did not get the means for working our lands. The few things they gave us did little good.

Our rations began to be reduced. They said we were lazy. That is false. How does any man of sense suppose that so great a number of people could get work at once unless they were at once supplied with the means to work and instructors enough to teach them?

Our ponies were taken away from us under the promise that they would be replaced by oxen and large horses. It was long before we saw any, and then we got very few. We tried with the means we had, but on for one reason or another, we were shifted from one place to another, or were told that such a transfer was coming. Great efforts were made to break up our customs, but nothing was done to introduce us to customs of the whites. Everything was done to break up the power of the real chiefs.

Name _____

Statement on the Causes of Wounded Knee—Divided Reading (cont.)

Group 3

Those old men really wished their people to improve, but little men, so-called chiefs, were made to act as disturbers and agitators. Spotted Tail wanted the ways of the whites, but an assassin was found to remove him. This was charged to the Indians because an Indian did it, but who set on the Indian? I was abused and slandered, to weaken my influence for good. This was done by men paid by the government to teach us the ways of the whites. I have visited many other tribes and found that the same things were done amongst them. All was done to discourage us and nothing to encourage us. I saw men paid by the government to help us, all very busy making money for themselves, but doing nothing for us . . .

Name _____

Statement on the Causes of
Wounded Knee—Divided Reading (cont.)

Group 4

The men who counted us told all around that we were feasting and wasting food. Where did he see it? How could we waste what we did not have? We felt we were mocked in our misery. We had no newspaper and no one to speak for us. Our rations were again reduced.

You who eat three times a day and see your children well and happy around you cannot understand what a starving Indian feels! We were faint with hunger and maddened by despair. We held our dying children and felt their little bodies tremble as their soul went out and left only a dead weight in our hands. They were not very heavy but we were faint and the dead weighed us down. There was no hope on Earth. God seemed to have forgotten.

Someone had been talking of the Son of God and said He had come. The people did not know. They did not care. They snatched at hope. They screamed like crazy people to Him for mercy. They caught at the promise they heard He had made.

Name _____

Statement on the Causes of Wounded Knee—Divided Reading (cont.)

Group 5

The white people were frightened and called for soldiers. We begged for life and the white men thought we wanted theirs. We heard the soldiers were coming. We did not fear. We hoped we could tell them our suffering and could get help. The white men told us the soldiers meant to kill us. We did not believe it but some were frightened and ran away to the Badlands. The soldiers came. They said: "Don't be afraid—we come to make peace, not war." It was true, they brought us food. But the hunger-crazed who had taken fright at the soldiers' coming and went to the Badlands could not be induced to return to the horrors of reservation life. They were called hostiles and the government sent the army to force them back to their reservation prison.

Abolitionists

Objective

√ Students will read passages fluently and accurately within a cumulative choral-reading activity, focusing on correct conversational and expressive language.

Preparation

- Make an overhead transparency of *"John Brown's Body"—Cumulative Choral Reading* (pages 74–75) and also copy the pages for each student.
- For optional use, copy *SCAMPER with John Brown* (page 76) for each student.

Fluency Suggestions and Activities

You may want to complete the history and vocabulary activities on the following page before starting this fluency activity. An understanding of the historical context and vocabulary will help students analyze and read the piece fluently.

Note: You might want to have students perform this reading around October 16, the date that John Brown and his men began the raid on Harper's Ferry.

1. Place a transparency copy of *"John Brown's Body"—Cumulative Choral Reading* (pages 74–75) on the overhead. Read it aloud, modeling fluent reading. Tell students that they will be reading this song for some of the staff members in the school.

2. Distribute copies of *"John Brown's Body"—Cumulative Choral Reading* to students. Read through the poem slowly, as a choral reading with the entire class. After each stanza, stop and look for clues in the text that tell you how to read it (e.g., commas, exclamation marks, periods, or repetition).

3. Then, explain what a cumulative choral reading is to the class. You will be dividing the class into six groups. Each group will be assigned one stanza. Within each group, one student will begin reading the poem. Then after one line, another student will join reading. The whole group of four readers will read the chorus together.

4. To begin, you will need to break the students into six groups. Assign stanzas to the students and give them a chance to practice. There are four lines in each stanza. If your groups are larger or smaller than four, you'll need to adjust how they should complete the cumulative part of the reading. In other words, if they have only three readers, they may choose to all read the last line together or one student could read the first two lines alone.

5. Give students plenty of time to practice their parts. Invite some of the staff (secretaries, music, art, and P.E. teachers) from the school into your classroom for your final performance.

Abolitionists *(cont.)*

History Connection

Introduce "John Brown's Body" using the information provided below.

This song was originally written about a Scottish volunteer soldier from Massachusetts by the name of John Brown. His friends constantly teased him because he had the same name as John Brown, the abolitionist. As they marched, they sang about their friend. The song became popular and new verses were added to apply to the abolitionist. John Brown, the abolitionist, was from Kansas. In 1859, he led a group of 18 people on a raid to an arsenal and rifle factory in Harper's Ferry, Virginia. He wanted to spark a slave rebellion. They barricaded themselves inside for two days with 10 prisoners. Under the command of Robert E. Lee, United States soldiers stormed the building and captured John Brown. He was convicted of treason and hanged just two months later. The song has many different versions, and as the war progressed, more verses were added. It was sung by Union troops to the same tune as "The Battle Hymn of the Republic."

Vocabulary Connection

Discuss unfamiliar vocabulary encountered in the text. Some possible words are listed below. After identifying the difficult words, discuss them within the context of the text.

- **a-moldering**—decaying
- **ventured**—a risky undertaking
- **undaunted**—fearless
- **valor**—courage
- **bondsman**—a slave
- **heralded**—to proclaim, to tell
- **anthems**—songs of praise

Extension Ideas

- Teach students the tune to "The Battle Hymn of the Republic." Have students practice singing "John Brown's Body" to this tune. Then, have students come up with other tunes that the song can be sung to and allow the class to practice. Have students analyze the effectiveness of the song depending on what beat and tune is used.

- Have students complete the activity sheet, *SCAMPER with John Brown* (page 76). This page asks students to apply what they know about the song and John Brown in a creative way.

Name _____

"John Brown's Body"— Cumulative Choral Reading

Old John Brown's body lies a-moldering in the grave,
While weep the sons of bondage whom he ventured all to save;
But though he lost his life in struggling for the slave,
His truth is marching on.

Glory, Glory! Hallelujah!
Glory, Glory! Hallelujah!
Glory, Glory! Hallelujah!
His soul is marching on

John Brown was a hero, undaunted, true and brave;
Kansas knew his valor when he fought her rights to save;
And now though the grass grows green above his grave,
His truth is marching on.

Glory, Glory! Hallelujah!
Glory, Glory! Hallelujah!
Glory, Glory! Hallelujah!
His soul is marching on

He captured Harper's Ferry with his nineteen men so few,
And he frightened "Old Virginny" till she trembled through and through,
They hung him for a traitor, themselves a traitor crew,
But his truth is marching on.

Glory, Glory! Hallelujah!
Glory, Glory! Hallelujah!
Glory, Glory! Hallelujah!
His soul is marching on

"John Brown's Body"— Cumulative Choral Reading *(cont.)*

John Brown was John the Baptist for the Christ we are to see,
Christ who of the bondsman shall the Liberator be;
And soon throughout the sunny South the slaves shall all be free.
For his truth is marching on.

Glory, Glory! Hallelujah!
Glory, Glory! Hallelujah!
Glory, Glory! Hallelujah!
His soul is marching on

The conflict that he heralded, he looks from heaven to view,
On the army of the Union with its flag, red, white, and blue,
And heaven shall ring with anthems o'er the deeds they mean to do,
For his truth is marching on.

Glory, Glory! Hallelujah!
Glory, Glory! Hallelujah!
Glory, Glory! Hallelujah!
His soul is marching on

Oh, soldiers of freedom, then strike while strike you may
The deathblow of oppression in a better time and way;
For the dawn of old John Brown was brightened into day,
And his truth is marching on.

Glory, Glory! Hallelujah!
Glory, Glory! Hallelujah!
Glory, Glory! Hallelujah!
His soul is marching on

Name _____

SCAMPER with John Brown

Directions: Use the song, "John Brown's Body," and what you know about John Brown the abolitionist to answer the questions below.

Substitute

Suppose you were at Harper's Ferry when this rebellion occurred. Write two verses of your own song that tell about John Brown.

Combine

Add another verse to the song. It can apply to the abolitionist or to the Scotsman.

Adapt

What parts of the song would have to be changed to make it still apply to the Scotsman, John Brown?

Modify

What if the newspapers had never printed the stories of John Brown and a song had never been written? How would people have heard about this rebellion back then? If it happened today, how would the public hear about it?

Put to Other Uses

Soldiers marched to this tune on their way to battle. List at least two other reasons someone could have for singing this song back then?

Eliminate

Imagine you were the publisher of this song. There is one verse that you don't like and want to take out. Which verse is it? Justify your reasons for removing it by writing to the songwriter.

Reverse

What if John Brown had not been hanged? How would John Brown's reputation have changed? Could this have prevented the Civil War from ever happening? Or, could it have changed the Civil War's outcome? Draw a picture that explains your answers.

To Arms in Dixie

Objective

√ Students will perform a song for two voices fluently with changes in tone, voice, timing, and expression.

Preparation

- Make an overhead transparency of the song, "Dixie" (pages 79–80).
- Copy *"Dixie"—A Song for Two Voices* (pages 81–83) for each student.
- For optional use, copy *"Dixie" by Dan Emmett* (page 84) for each student.

Fluency Suggestions and Activities

You may want to complete the history and vocabulary activities on the following page before starting this fluency activity. An understanding of the historical context and vocabulary will help students analyze and read the piece fluently.

1. Place the transparency of the song, "Dixie" (pages 79–80), on the overhead and read it aloud for the students, modeling fluent reading. Ask them to offer their thoughts about what the poem means. If possible, play the music to this song and let students sing along.

2. Explain to the students that they will all have the opportunity to read this song aloud in pairs. Arrange to have each pair of students present the song for a different class or audience within the school. (You could put up a sign-up sheet in the teachers' lounge and ask for teachers who are willing to have your students visit their classrooms.)

3. Distribute copies of *"Dixie"—A Song for Two Voices* (pages 81–83) and draw the students' attention to the layout of the words of the song. Explain that the song is divided into parts for Voice 1 and Voice 2. Voice 1 begins the reading because the first line of the poem is below that heading. The next line is under the heading Voice 2. Some lines of the poem are read together. These lines are bolded.

4. Encourage students to focus on voice tone, timing, and facial expressions as they read. Discuss with students how their tones of voice can affect the mood of the song. Discuss how the speed at which they read is important, as well. Emphasize to the students that because people will be watching them perform, it is important to think about their facial expressions.

5. Invite two students to model reading a few lines of the song for the class. Tell the students that this kind of poem takes practice to read fluently. Divide the students into pairs and tell them that they will be performing this piece for another class in the school.

6. Allow the students time to practice their parts. They should practice their parts in the classroom on the day of the presentations, too.

To Arms in Dixie (cont.)

History Connection

Introduce "Dixie" using the information provided below.

In 1859, the first version of "Dixie" was written by Dan Emmet as a comic melody to entertain audiences. When the war broke out, a man by the name of General Albert Pike took the melody and rewrote the song to suit the South. He used the words to call the South to arms. It did inspire Confederate soldiers and they went to battle singing it. Soon it became the most loved song of the Confederacy.

Vocabulary Connection

Discuss unfamiliar vocabulary encountered in the text. Some possible words are listed below. After identifying the difficult words, discuss them within the context of the text.

- **Southrons**—Southerners
- **defiance**—to resist boldly
- **accursed**—cursed
- **alliance**—a close association
- **shun**—to turn away
- **pike**—a weapon used by a soldier with a metal spearhead and a long wooden handle
- **saber**—a heavy cavalry sword with a curved blade
- **betrayed**—failed in time of need
- **asunder**—separate into pieces
- **plunder**—to attack and steal from
- **falter**—to stumble
- **exultant**—triumphant
- **spoilers**—a group that has little chance of winning
- **Federation**—the Confederacy

Extension Idea

- Tell students that there are many versions to this song. Have students look at the earliest copy of the song on the activity page *"Dixie" by Dan Emmett* (page 84). Then, have them compare the two versions of the song using the Venn diagram on that page.

Dixie

By General Albert Pike

Southrons, hear your country call you!
Up, lest worse than death befall you!
To arms! To arms! To arms! In Dixie!
Lo! All the beacon-fires are lighted
Let all hearts be now united!
To arms! To arms! To arms! In Dixie!

Chorus:
Advance the flag of Dixie
Hurrah! Hurrah!
For Dixie's Land we take our stand,
And live or die for Dixie!
To Arms! To Arms!
And conquer peace for Dixie!

Hear the Northern thunders mutter!
Northern flags in South winds flutter!
To arms! To arms! To arms! In Dixie!
Send them back your fierce defiance!
Stamp upon the accursed alliance!
To arms! To arms! To arms! In Dixie!

Repeat Chorus

Fear no danger! Shun no labor!
Lift up rifle, pike, and saber!
To arms! To arms! To arms! In Dixie!
Shoulder pressing close to shoulder,
Let the odds make each heart bolder!
To arms! To arms! To arms! In Dixie!

Repeat Chorus

How the South's great heart rejoices
At your cannon's ringing voices!
To arms! To arms! To arms! In Dixie!
For faith betrayed and pledges broken,
Wrongs inflicted, insults spoken,
To arms! To arms! To arms! In Dixie!

Dixie (cont.)

Repeat Chorus

Strong as lions, swift as eagles,
Back to their kennels hunt these beagles!
To arms! To arms! To arms! In Dixie!
Cut the unequal bond asunder!
Let them hence each other plunder!
To arms! To arms! To arms! In Dixie!

Repeat Chorus

Swear upon your country's altar
Never to submit or to falter!
To arms! To arms! To arms! In Dixie!
Till the spoilers are defeated,
Till the Lord's work is completed,
To arms! To arms! To arms! In Dixie!

Repeat Chorus

Halt not till our Federation
Secures among earth's powers its station!
To arms! To arms! To arms! In Dixie!
Then at peace, and crowned with glory,
Hear your children tell the story!
To arms! To arms! To arms! In Dixie!

Repeat Chorus

If the loved ones weep in sadness,
Victory soon shall bring them gladness.
To arms! To arms! To arms! In Dixie!
Exultant pride soon banish sorrow;
Smiles chase tears away tomorrow.
To arms! To arms! To arms! In Dixie!

Repeat Chorus

Name _____

"Dixie"—A Song for Two Voices

Voice 1	Voice 2
Southrons, hear your country call you!	
	Up, lest worse than death befall you!
To arms! To arms! To arms! In Dixie!	**To arms! To arms! To arms! In Dixie!**
Lo! All the beacon fires are lighted	
	Let all hearts be now united!
To arms! To arms! To arms! In Dixie!	**To arms! To arms! To arms! In Dixie!**
Hear the Northern thunders mutter!	
	Northern flags in South winds flutter!
To arms! To arms! To arms! In Dixie!	**To arms! To arms! To arms! In Dixie!**
Send them back your fierce defiance!	
	Stamp upon the accursed alliance!
To arms! To arms! To arms! In Dixie!	**To arms! To arms! To arms! In Dixie!**
Advance the flag of Dixie!	
For Dixie's Land we take our stand,	Hurrah! Hurrah!
	And live or die for Dixie!
To arms! To arms! **And conquer peace for Dixie!**	**To arms! To arms!** **And conquer peace for Dixie!**
Fear no danger! Shun no labor!	
	Lift up rifle, pike, and saber!
To arms! To arms! To arms! In Dixie!	**To arms! To arms! To arms! In Dixie!**
Shoulder pressing close to shoulder,	
	Let the odds make each heart bolder!
To arms! To arms! To arms! In Dixie!	**To arms! To arms! To arms! In Dixie!**

"Dixie"—A Song for Two Voices (cont.)

Voice 1

How the South's great heart rejoices

To arms! To arms! To arms! In Dixie!

For faith betrayed and pledges broken,

To arms! To arms! To arms! In Dixie!

Advance the flag of Dixie!

For Dixie's Land we take our stand,

To arms! To arms!
And conquer peace for Dixie!

Strong as lions, swift as eagles,

To arms! To arms! To arms! In Dixie!

Cut the unequal bond asunder!

To arms! To arms! To arms! In Dixie!

Swear upon your country's altar

To arms! To arms! To arms! In Dixie!

Till the spoilers are defeated,

To arms! To arms! To arms! In Dixie!

Voice 2

At your cannon's ringing voices!

To arms! To arms! To arms! In Dixie!

Wrongs inflicted, insults spoken,

To arms! To arms! To arms! In Dixie!

Hurrah! Hurrah!

And live or die for Dixie!

To arms! To arms!
And conquer peace for Dixie!

Back to their kennels hunt these beagles!

To arms! To arms! To arms! In Dixie!

Let them hence each other plunder!

To arms! To arms! To arms! In Dixie!

Never to submit or to falter!

To arms! To arms! To arms! In Dixie!

Till the Lord's work is completed,

To arms! To arms! To arms! In Dixie!

"Dixie"—A Song for Two Voices (cont.)

Voice 1	**Voice 2**
Advance the flag of Dixie!	
	Hurrah! Hurrah!
For Dixie's Land we take our stand,	
	And live or die for Dixie!
To arms! To arms! **And conquer peace for Dixie!**	**To arms! To arms!** **And conquer peace for Dixie!**
Halt not till our Federation	
	Secures among earth's powers its station!
To arms! To arms! To arms! In Dixie!	**To arms! To arms! To arms! In Dixie!**
Then at peace, and crowned with glory,	
	Hear your children tell the story!
To arms! To arms! To arms! In Dixie!	**To arms! To arms! To arms! In Dixie!**
If the loved ones weep in sadness,	
	Victory soon shall bring them gladness.
To arms! To arms! To arms! In Dixie!	**To arms! To arms! To arms! In Dixie!**
Exultant pride soon banish sorrow;	
	Smiles chase tears away tomorrow.
To arms! To arms! To arms! In Dixie!	**To arms! To arms! To arms! In Dixie!**
Advance the flag of Dixie!	
	Hurrah! Hurrah!
For Dixie's Land we take our stand,	
	And live or die for Dixie!
To arms! To arms! **And conquer peace for Dixie!**	**To arms! To arms!** **And conquer peace for Dixie!**

Name _____

"Dixie" by Dan Emmett

I wish I was in de land of cotton,
Old times dar am not forgotten;
Look away! Look away! Look away! Dixie Land.
In Dixie Land whar I was born in,
Early on one frosty mornin,
Look away! Look away! Look away! Dixie Land.

Den I wish I was in Dixie, Hooray! Hooray!
In Dixie Land, I'll take my stand, To lib and die in Dixie,
Away, away, away down south in Dixie,
Away, away, away down south in Dixie.

Dar's buck-wheat cakes and 'Ingen'batter,
Makes you fat or a little fatter;
Look away! Look away! Look away! Dixie Land.
Den hoe it down and scratch your grabble,
To Dixie land I'm bound to trabble.
Look away! Look away! Look away! Dixie Land.

Directions: Above is the earliest copy of the song, "Dixie." Use the Venn diagram below to compare this version with the more common version. Compare their messages, audiences (who they were written for), and who the songs were written about.

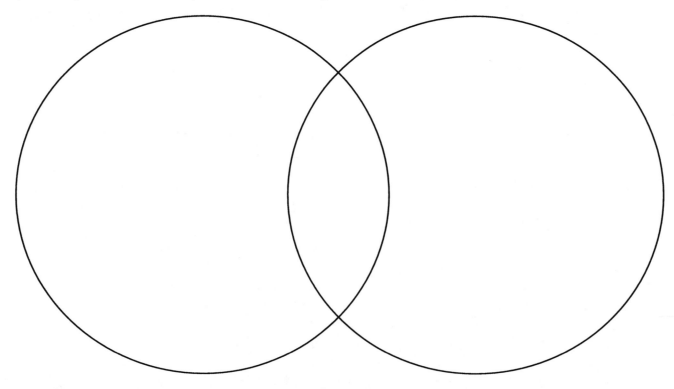

Sherman's March

Objective

√ Students will deliver a group oral presentation and read passages fluently with changes in tone, voice, timing, and expression using echo reading.

Preparation

- Copy the song, "Marching through Georgia" (page 87), for each student.
- Copy *"Marching through Georgia"—Echo Reading* (pages 88–89) for each student.
- For optional use, copy *Sherman's Advice* (page 90) for each student.

Fluency Suggestions and Activities

You may want to complete the history and vocabulary activities on the following page before starting this fluency activity. An understanding of the historical context and vocabulary will help students analyze and read the piece fluently.

1. Give students a copy of the song, "Marching through Georgia" (page 87). Read it aloud, modeling fluent reading. If possible, have students listen to a recording of the song after your reading.

2. Read the poem as an echo reading with the class. You read two lines and the students read them back to you. Continue until you have read the entire poem.

3. Ask students to look for clues in the text that tell them how to read it (e.g. commas, exclamation marks, periods, or repetition).

4. Place the students into groups consisting of four people each. Each group will be responsible for presenting an echo reading to the class. Then, the class will vote on which group gave the most energetic and interesting performance. Tell the groups to choose a point of view when presenting the song. One view is from the Northern perspective and the other view is from the Southern perspective. This will give them real reasons for the tones and inflections they will use.

5. Once the students are in their groups, give them copies of *"Marching through Georgia"—Echo Reading* (pages 88–89). This sheet has the piece broken into echo reading parts for four students.

6. On the day of the presentations, have each group perform its echo reading. Encourage students to use hand motions and facial expressions as they read. Remind them that they want to get the audience involved in the presentation of the song. Then, after all the groups have presented, take a vote on which group gave the most energetic and interesting performance. You might want to tell students that they cannot vote for their own groups.

Sherman's March *(cont.)*

History Connection

Introduce "Marching through Georgia" using the information provided below.

A man by the name of Henry Clay Work wrote "Marching through Georgia" in 1865 as a result of General William Sherman's "March to the Sea." It became extremely popular. General Sherman complained that he heard it everywhere he went, even in Europe. Just before Sherman died, he had to listen to it play for seven hours straight. He promised never to attend another national ceremony unless they promise to not play the song. Six months later, the tune was played in his presence, but he could not hear it. It was the ceremony for his funeral.

Vocabulary Connection

Discuss unfamiliar vocabulary encountered in the text. Some possible words are listed below. After identifying the difficult words, discuss them within the context of the text.

- **darkeys**—slaves
- **commissary**—person in charge of gathering food for the soldiers
- **restrained**—held back
- **saucy**—bold
- **thoroughfare**—main road
- **latitude**—the lines that run east and west on the globe
- **treason**—traitors or Southerners

Extension Idea

- Ask students to imagine they have the opportunity to talk with General Sherman about this song. Distribute copies of *Sherman's Advice* (page 90). Have students work with partners to complete the activities on that page. If possible, allow students to present their new verses to the class.

Marching through Georgia

By Henry Clay Work

Bring the good ol' Bugle boys! We'll sing another song,
Sing it with a spirit that will start the world along,
Sing it like we used to sing it fifty thousand strong,
While we were marching through Georgia

Chorus:
Hurrah! Hurrah! We bring the Jubilee.
Hurrah! Hurrah! The flag that makes you free,
So we sang the chorus from Atlanta to the sea,
While we were marching through Georgia.

How the darkeys shouted when they heard the joyful sound,
How the turkeys gobbled which our commissary found,
How the sweet potatoes even started from the ground,
While we were marching through Georgia.

Repeat Chorus

Yes and there were Union men who wept with joyful tears,
When they saw the honored flag they had not seen for years;
Hardly could they be restrained from breaking forth in cheers,
While we were marching through Georgia.

Repeat Chorus

"Sherman's dashing Yankee boys will never make the coast!"
So the saucy rebels said and 'twas a handsome boast
Had they not forgot, alas! to reckon with the Host
While we were marching through Georgia.

Repeat Chorus

So we made a thoroughfare for freedom and her train,
Sixty miles of latitude, three hundred to the main;
Treason fled before us, for resistance was in vain
While we were marching through Georgia.

Repeat Chorus

Name _____

"Marching through Georgia"— Echo Reading

Student 1
Bring the good old Bugle boys! We'll sing another song,
Sing it with a spirit that will start the world along,
(audience echos)

Student 2
Sing it like we used to sing it 50 thousand strong,
While we were marching through Georgia
(audience echos)

All
Hurrah! Hurrah! We bring the Jubilee.
Hurrah! Hurrah! The flag that makes you free,
So we sang the chorus from Atlanta to the sea,
While we were marching through Georgia.

Student 3
How the darkeys shouted when they heard the joyful sound,
How the turkeys gobbled which our commissary found,
(audience echos)

Student 4
How the sweet potatoes even started from the ground,
While we were marching through Georgia.
(audience echos)

All
Hurrah! Hurrah! We bring the Jubilee.
Hurrah! Hurrah! The flag that makes you free,
So we sang the chorus from Atlanta to the sea,
While we were marching through Georgia.

Student 1
Yes and there were Union men who wept with joyful tears,
When they saw the honored flag they had not seen for years;
(audience echos)

Student 2
Hardly could they be restrained from breaking forth in cheers,
While we were marching through Georgia.
(audience echos)

"Marching through Georgia"— Echo Reading *(cont.)*

All
Hurrah! Hurrah! We bring the Jubilee.
Hurrah! Hurrah! The flag that makes you free,
So we sang the chorus from Atlanta to the sea,
While we were marching through Georgia.

Student 3
"Sherman's dashing Yankee boys will never make the coast!"
So the saucy rebels said and 'twas a handsome boast
(audience echos)

Student 4
Had they not forgot, alas! to reckon with the Host
While we were marching through Georgia.
(audience echos)

All
Hurrah! Hurrah! We bring the Jubilee.
Hurrah! Hurrah! The flag that makes you free,
So we sang the chorus from Atlanta to the sea,
While we were marching through Georgia.

Students 1 and 2
So we made a thoroughfare for freedom and her train,
Sixty miles of latitude, 300 to the main;
(audience echos)

Students 3 and 4
Treason fled before us, for resistance was in vain
While we were marching through Georgia.
(audience echos)

All
Hurrah! Hurrah! We bring the Jubilee.
Hurrah! Hurrah! The flag that makes you free,
So we sang the chorus from Atlanta to the sea,
While we were marching through Georgia.

Name _____

Sherman's Advice

Directions: Imagine that you had the opportunity to consult General William Sherman about this song. Answer the questions below.

1. You find out that General Sherman doesn't like the song. Look back at the lyrics. Why do you think he doesn't like it?

   _____

   _____

   _____

2. What are the best elements of the song? How can you convince Sherman to keep that part of the song?

   _____

   _____

   _____

3. Sherman wants you to write a new verse to the song. Write it below. How does this new verse make this song better?

   _____

   _____

   _____

4. Read this song twice to a partner. On the first reading, read as if you were a Northerner. On the second reading, read as if you were a Southerner. Have your partner list any changes in your tone, volume, or reading rate in the chart below.

Character	Tone	Volume	Reading Rate
Northerner			
Southerner			

Following Jackson

Objective

√ Students will read passages fluently and accurately within a paired-reading activity.

Preparation

- Copy the song, "Stonewall Jackson's Way" (page 93), for each student.
- Copy the *Fluency Evaluation* (page 94) for each student.
- Gather blank tapes and tape recorders.

Fluency Suggestions and Activities

You may want to complete the history and vocabulary activities on the following page before starting this fluency activity. An understanding of the historical context and vocabulary will help students analyze and read the piece fluently.

1. Distribute and introduce the song, "Stonewall Jackson's Way" (page 93). Model an expressive reading of the text.

2. Tell students that they will be reading this song into a tape recorder. These tapes will be placed in the library for others to listen to and read along with. Be sure to place a copy of the song with the recorded tape so that others can practice their fluent reading, too.

3. Divide the students into pairs. Try to pair a low reader (partner A) with a high reader (partner B). Have the students read the selection within their pairs. The "B" partners should read alone first. These are the stronger students, and by reading first, they are modeling fluent reading of the passage.

4. The "A" partners are more likely going to have difficulty reading the passage fluently. They should follow along on a printed copy of the text while listening to the "B" partner read. Then, the two students can read the passage together. Finally, the "A" partner can read the selection independently with help from the fluent reader.

5. For the actual performances that will be taped, each pair can decide how to read the piece. They can each read stanzas alone, or they can read the song together. They can even mix it up and read both individually and together. After several opportunities to read the text, set up a tape recorder with a blank tape for each paired group. Allow each group to decide how they want to tape themselves reading. They can do this together or individually.

6. Distribute copies of the *Fluency Evaluation* (page 94) to students. Have them evaluate their taped performance using this page.

Following Jackson (cont.)

History Connection

Introduce "Stonewall Jackson" using the information provided below.

Thomas Jackson earned the name "Stonewall" at the Battle of First Manassas in 1861. His brigade halted the Union army from advancing and the battle turned into a victory for the Confederates. Supposedly, a Confederate soldier saw Jackson and his men holding the line and exclaimed, "There is Jackson, standing like a stone wall!" As a general, Jackson was both feared and respected throughout the North and the South. He had peculiar mannerisms and was extremely religious. He expected his men to win battles, and they did. A little over a year after this battle, John Williamson Palmer wrote this song.

Vocabulary Connection

Discuss unfamiliar vocabulary encountered in the text. Some possible words are listed below. After identifying the difficult words, discuss them within the context of the text.

- **arms**—weapons
- **canteen**—container for holding liquids
- **rousing**—brisk or lively
- **slouched hat**—soft felt hat with a wide brim
- **cocked**—set at a slant
- **askew**—not exactly straight
- **shrewd**—clever
- **scoff**—to make fun
- *in forma pauperis*—in the form of a pauper; as a poor person
- **lists**—fields of battle
- **hemmed**—confined or stuck
- **gorge**—a narrow passageway through land
- **yearn**—to long for or want
- **forlorn**—sad and lonely

Extension Idea

- What if the words to this song became a play? Have students work in small groups to choose a scene (i.e., a stanza) they would like to act out. As one student reads the chosen scene from the song, the others will silently act out the scene. This will also encourage students to practice reading fluently and with expression. Provide enough time for students to practice their actions, and then let them show their scenes to the class.

Stonewall Jackson's Way

By John Williamson Palmer

Come, stack arms, men! Pile on the rails,
Stir up the campfire bright;
No matter if the canteen fails,
We'll make a roaring night.
Here Shenandoah brawls along,
There burly Blue Ridge echoes strong
To swell the brigade's rousing song
Of "Stonewall Jackson's way."

We see him now, the old slouched hat
Cocked o'er his eye askew,
The shrewd, dry smile, the speech so pat,
So calm, so blunt, so true.
That "Blue-Light Elder" knows 'em well
Says he, "That's Banks, he's fond of shell
Lord save his soul! we'll give him" . . . well,
That's "Stonewall Jackson's way."

Silence! Ground arms! Kneel all! Caps off!
Old Blue Light's going to pray;
Strangle the fool that dares to scoff;
Attention, it's his way.
Appealing from his native sod,
In forma pauperis to God—
"Lay bare thine arm; stretch forth thy rod;
Amen." That's "Stonewall's way."

He's in the saddle now! Fall in!
Steady, the whole brigade!
Hill's at the ford, cut off! He'll win
His way out, ball and blade.
What matter if our shoes are worn?
What matter if our feet are torn?
"Quick-step—we're with him before morn!"
That's "Stonewall Jackson's way."

The sun's bright glances rout the mists
Of morning, and, by George!
There's Longstreet struggling in the lists,
Hemmed in an ugly gorge—
Pope and his Yankees whipped before,
"Bayonet and grape!" hear Stonewall roar,
"Charge, Stuart! Pay off Ashby's score."
In "Stonewall Jackson's way."

Ah, maiden! Wait and watch and yearn
For news of Stonewall's band!
Ah, widow! Read with eyes that burn
That ring upon thy hand!
Ah, wife! Sew on, pray on, hope on,
Thy life shall not be all forlorn
The foe had better ne'er been born
That gets in "Stonewall's way."

Fluency Evaluation

Directions: Practice reading the song, "Stonewall Jackson's Way." Ask for help with reading any words that are unfamiliar to you. Record your performance of the passage. Then, listen to the recording and complete this page to evaluate your reading fluency.

Names: _____

Our reading was:	very smooth	somewhat smooth	choppy
Our reading rate was:	too slow	just right	too fast

We made mistakes reading these words: _____

Did we use expression?   Yes   No

Here is our plan for improvement: _____

_____

_____

Directions: Practice reading the passage and record yourself again. Then, complete the evaluation again to compare your two recordings.

Our reading was:	very smooth	somewhat smooth	choppy
Our reading rate was:	too slow	just right	too fast

We made mistakes reading these words: _____

Did we use expression?   Yes   No

Here is how our reading fluency changed: _____

_____

_____

Glory! Glory! Hallelujah!

Objective

√ Students will read aloud fluently and accurately with changes in tone, voice, timing, and expression using the strategy of choral reading.

Preparation

- Copy the song, "Battle Hymn of the Republic" (page 97), for each student.
- Copy *"Battle Hymn of the Republic"—Choral Reading* (page 98) for each student.
- Copy *Elements of Fluency* (page 99) for each student.
- Make copies of *Oral Reading Fluency Evaluation* (page 100) for the guests.

Fluency Suggestions and Activities

You may want to complete the history and vocabulary activities on the following page before starting this fluency activity. An understanding of the historical context and vocabulary will help students analyze and read the piece fluently.

Note: You might want students to complete this reading activity around the birthday of the songwriter, Julia Howe, on May 27.

1. Distributes copies of the song, "Battle Hymn of the Republic" (page 97), to the students. Read the song, modeling fluent reading. Explain to the students that developing fluency isn't just about practicing one's own fluent reading. It also involves listening to other readers.

2. If possible, have students sing the song as a class. Then, read the song with the entire class as a choral reading.

3. Next, have children get into small groups of four or five and practice reading the song chorally. Then, read the song again with the entire class reading it together.

4. Distribute *"Battle Hymn of the Republic"—Choral Reading* (page 98). Draw the students' attention to the special lines throughout this piece such as, "His truth is marching on." Model how you want students to read these lines. Use a great deal of expression and change the volume for a dramatic effect. First read these lines in a whispering volume, then read again a little louder, and then finish with a loud, bolstering volume.

5. Give students ample time to practice reading the speech in their small groups using the technique explained above. Copy and distribute *Elements of Fluency* (page 99) for the students. Tell them that their audience will use these questions to evaluate the class performance.

6. Finally, arrange ahead of time for students to perform a full-class reading of the song for another class. Give the other class copies of *Oral Reading Fluency Evaluation* (page 100). Instruct them to read it before the performance and to fill it out after the performance. Collect these pages and review them with your class.

Glory! Glory! Hallelujah! (cont.)

History Connection

Introduce "Battle Hymn of the Republic" using the information provided below.

Julia Ward Howe, the wife of a government official, attended a military review in Virginia. She rode with her pastor to the event. He heard her singing "John Brown's Body" and suggested that she might be able to find better words for the melody. That very evening, she wrote the words to a poem. She sold it to *Atlantic Monthly* magazine for just five dollars. They gave her poem the title, "Battle Hymn of the Republic." It became an anthem for the Union.

Vocabulary Connection

Discuss unfamiliar vocabulary encountered in the text. Some possible words are listed below. After identifying the difficult words, discuss them within the context of the text.

- **trampling**—crushing by stomping on something
- **vintage**—crops of grapes
- **wrath**—anger
- **righteous**—morally right
- **burnished**—polished
- **contemners**—those who treat others with hatred
- **jubilant**—happy
- **transfigures**—transforms spiritually

Extension Idea

- Have students think about the images that they see in their heads as they read this piece. Place a large sheet of paper on the wall and allow students to create a mural of images for this song. This might create a great background display for the reading presentation.

Battle Hymn of the Republic

By Julia Ward Howe

Mine eyes have seen the glory of the coming of the Lord;
He is trampling out the vintage where the grapes of wrath are stored;
He hath loosed the fateful lightning of His terrible swift sword,
His truth is marching on.

Chorus:
Glory! Glory! Hallelujah!
Glory! Glory! Hallelujah!
Glory! Glory! Hallelujah!
His truth is marching on.

I have seen Him in the watch-fires of a hundred circling camps;
They have builded Him an altar in the evening dews and damps;
I can read His righteous sentence by the dim and flaring lamps,
His day is marching on.

Repeat Chorus

I have read a fiery gospel, writ in burnished rows of steel;
"As ye deal with My contemners, so with you My grace shall deal;
Let the Hero, born of woman, crush the serpent with his heel,
Since God is marching on."

Repeat Chorus

He has sounded forth the trumpet that shall never call retreat;
He is sifting out the hearts of men before His judgment seat;
Oh, be swift, my soul, to answer Him; be jubilant, my feet;
Our God is marching on.

Repeat Chorus

In the beauty of the lilies Christ was born across the sea,
With a glory in His bosom that transfigures you and me;
As He died to make men holy, let us die to make men free,
While God is marching on.

Repeat Chorus

Name _____

"Battle Hymn of the Republic"— Choral Reading

Mine eyes have seen the glory of the coming of the Lord;
  His truth is marching on.
He is trampling out the vintage where the grapes of wrath are stored;
  His truth is marching on.
He hath loosed the fateful lightning of His terrible swift sword,
  His truth is marching on.

I have seen Him in the watch-fires of a hundred circling camps;
  His day is marching on.
They have builded Him an altar in the evening dews and damps;
  His day is marching on.
I can read His righteous sentence by the dim and flaring lamps,
  His day is marching on.

I have read a fiery gospel, writ in burnished rows of steel;
  Since God is marching on.
"As ye deal with My contemners, so with you My grace shall deal;
  Since God is marching on.
Let the Hero born of woman crush the serpent with His heel,"
  Since God is marching on.

He has sounded forth the trumpet that shall never call retreat;
  Our God is marching on.
He is sifting out the hearts of men before His judgment seat;
  Our God is marching on.
Oh, be swift, my soul, to answer Him; be jubilant, my feet;
  Our God is marching on.

In the beauty of the lilies Christ was born across the sea,
  While God is marching on.
With a glory in His bosom that transfigures you and me;
  While God is marching on.
As He died to make men holy, let us die to make men free,
  While God is marching on.

Name _____

Elements of Fluency

Rate of Reading

- How is the speed of reading?
- Is it too fast? Is it too slow?
- Is the speed of the reading easy to understand?
- Is the reading speed distracting?

Loudness

- Is the reading too soft?
- Is the reading too loud?
- Is it just right?
- Does the loudness of the reading match the size of the audience?

Accuracy

- Do the readers pronounce the words correctly?
- Do the readers skip words?

Smoothness

- Is the reading smooth?
- Is the reading choppy?
- Do the readers speed up and slow down?

Expression

- Do the readers use expression?
- Do the expressions match the mood of the text?

Name _____

Oral Reading Fluency Evaluation

Directions: Listen to the class performance. Then, circle your choices below. Write your comments at the bottom of the page.

Rate of Reading

Too fast   Too slow   Just right

Easy to understand   Difficult to understand

Loudness

Too loud   Too soft   Just right

Matches audience size   Doesn't match audience size

Accuracy

Correct pronunciation   Many mispronounced words

Skipped words   Didn't skip words

Smoothness

Smooth reading   Choppy reading

Reading that speeds up and slows down

Reading smoothness just right

Expression

Expression   No expression

Expression matches text   Expression doesn't match text

Additional comments: _____

_____

_____

Marching Home from War

Objective

√ Students will perform a song for two voices with changes in tone, voice, timing, and expression.

Preparation

- Make an overhead transparency of the song, "When Johnny Comes Marching Home" (page 103).
- Copy *"When Johnny Comes Marching Home"—A Song for Two Voices* (page 104) for each student.

Fluency Suggestions and Activities

You may want to complete the history and vocabulary activities on the following page before starting this fluency activity. An understanding of the historical context and vocabulary will help students analyze and read the piece fluently.

Note: You might want to have students perform this piece in April to celebrate the anniversary of the end of the Civil War.

1. Place the transparency on the overhead and read the song, "When Johnny Comes Marching Home" (page 103), aloud to the students. Ask students if they know what it means to serenade someone. Explain that it usually means someone singing to another person. Tell students that they will be performing a reading serenade to other students in the school.

2. Read the song aloud together several times. Model reading lines with changes in pitch, tone, and timing to achieve different effects. Ask students to look for clues in the text that tell them how to read it (e.g., commas, periods, or exclamation points for emphasis).

3. Distribute *"When Johnny Comes Marching Home"—A Song for Two Voices* (page 104). Draw their attention to the way the words are divided into parts for Voice 1 and Voice 2. Voice 1 begins the reading because the first line of the poem is below that heading. The next line falls under the heading Voice 2. Some lines of the poem are read together, as they fall below both headings in the same place. These lines are indicated by bold text.

4. Next, divide the class into the two groups. Assign each group one of the "voices," and practice reading the song as a class with two voices.

5. Place the students into pairs. Then, allow time for students to work in their pairs to practice reading the song this way.

6. Ahead of time, arrange with the librarian and other teachers for your student pairs to perform their serenade readings in the library. Students should approach a reading table and ask the people sitting there for permission to read to them. This activity can take place over the time frame of a week, allowing a certain number of paired-students to serenade unsuspecting students in the library each day.

Marching Home from War *(cont.)*

History Connection

Introduce "When Johnny Comes Marching Home" using the information provided below.

Patrick Gilmore was an Irish immigrant who arrived in Boston in 1848. He was a bandmaster and his band enlisted in 1861 to fight with the Union forces. His band not only played music for the marching troops, they also carried the stretchers of wounded men off the battlefield. In 1863, he was sent to New Orleans, Louisiana, to be the Grand Master of the Union army. It was there that he reorganized the state military bands and wrote "When Johnny Comes Marching Home." Men from both the Union and Confederacy sang this song as they marched. The people at home sang it as they looked forward to loved ones returning from the war.

Vocabulary Connection

Discuss unfamiliar vocabulary encountered in the text. Some possible words are listed below. After identifying the difficult words, discuss them within the context of the text.

- **hearty**—warm and friendly, enthusiastic
- **gay**—happy
- **peal**—ring
- **lads**—boys
- **lassies**—girls
- **strew**—to scatter along
- **laurel wreath**—a type of tree leaf used for decorations
- **brow**—forehead

Extension Idea

- Have students create a story in the first person about someone coming home from war. What were they expecting to find after being gone for so long? Did they find what they were expecting? Had people changed and in what ways? Copy these stories and have students form literature circles. Allow students to read these stories in their literature circles. They can also write some discussion questions about their stories and use them in their circles.

When Johnny Comes Marching Home

By Patrick Gilmore

When Johnny comes marching home again,
Hurrah! Hurrah!
We'll give him a hearty welcome then,
Hurrah! Hurrah!
The men will cheer, the boys will shout,
The ladies they will all turn out,
And we'll all feel gay
When Johnny comes marching home.

The old church bell will peal with joy,
Hurrah! Hurrah!
To welcome home our darling boy,
Hurrah! Hurrah!
The village lads and lassies say
With roses they will strew the way,
And we'll all feel gay
When Johnny comes marching home.

Get ready for the Jubilee,
Hurrah! Hurrah!
We'll give the hero three times three,
Hurrah! Hurrah!
The laurel wreath is ready now
To place upon his loyal brow,
And we'll all feel gay
When Johnny comes marching home.

Let love and friendship on that day,
Hurrah! Hurrah!
Their choices treasures then display
Hurrah! Hurrah!
And let each one perform some part
To fill with joy the warrior's heart,
And we'll all feel gay
When Johnny comes marching home.

Name _____

"When Johnny Comes Marching Home"—A Song for Two Voices

Voice 1

When Johnny comes marching
home again, Hurrah! Hurrah!

The men will cheer, the boys will shout,

**And we'll all feel gay when Johnny
comes marching home.**

The old church bell will peal with joy,
Hurrah! Hurrah!

The village lads and lassies say

**And we'll all feel gay when Johnny
comes marching home.**

Get ready for the Jubilee,
Hurrah! Hurrah!

The laurel wreath is ready now

**And we'll all feel gay when Johnny
comes marching home.**

Let love and friendship on that day,
Hurrah! Hurrah!

And let each one perform some part

**And we'll all feel gay when Johnny
comes marching home.**

Voice 2

We'll give him a hearty welcome
then, Hurrah! Hurrah!

The ladies they will all turn out,

**And we'll all feel gay when Johnny
comes marching home.**

To welcome home our darling boy,
Hurrah! Hurrah!

With roses they will strew the way,

**And we'll all feel gay when Johnny
comes marching home.**

We'll give the hero three times three,
Hurrah! Hurrah!

To place upon his loyal brow,

**And we'll all feel gay when Johnny
comes marching home.**

Their choices treasures then display,
Hurrah! Hurrah!

To fill with joy the warrior's hear,

**And we'll all feel gay when Johnny
comes marching home.**

Lewis's Adventures

Objective

√ Students will participate in cooperative learning and improve expressive reading skills by engaging in reader's theater.

Preparation

- Make an overhead transparency of *Friday, June 14, 1805, Journal Entry* (page 107).
- Copy *Lewis and the Bear—Reader's Theater* (pages 108–110) for each student.
- Provide highlighters.

Fluency Suggestions and Activities

You may want to complete the history and vocabulary activities on the following page before starting this fluency activity. An understanding of the historical context and vocabulary will help students analyze and read the piece fluently.

Note: You might want to plan to complete this fluency activity around May 14 to celebrate the day the Corps of Discovery began their trip west.

1. Place the transparency of *Friday, June 14, 1805, Journal Entry* (page 107) on the overhead and model a fluent reading of the text. Tell students that they will be performing this journal entry as a reader's theater for a school-wide celebration commemorating the expedition of Lewis and Clark's Corps of Discovery. Work together with your principal and other teachers to plan this celebration during school hours. Other classes can read and write poems and songs or choreograph dances honoring this group of men.

2. Give each student a copy of *Lewis and the Bear—Reader's Theater* (pages 108–110). Read the script together several times. Model reading lines with changes in pitch, tone, and timing to achieve different effects. Ask students to look for clues in the text that tell them how to read it.

3. Then, place students into groups of five. Assign parts to students by having them volunteer or audition. Have students highlight their parts. All members of the group read the "All" lines together. Those lines are in bold to make them stand out.

4. Have students read their assigned parts aloud in their groups. Provide time for practice individually and in small groups.

5. Make sure students have enough time to practice reading their parts before the school-wide celebration.

Lewis's Adventures *(cont.)*

History Connection

Introduce Meriwether Lewis's journal using the information provided below.

In 1803, Thomas Jefferson made the best land deal ever! He purchased a piece of land called Louisiana from France. At this point, no one had explored the West, so Jefferson sent his secretary Meriwether Lewis and Lewis's friend, William Clark, on an expedition. Lewis was a very educated man. He studied about plants, animals, and medicine to help him prepare for the trip. They gathered a group of 40 men and called themselves the Corps of Discovery. Both Lewis and Clark kept journals of their expedition recording plants, animals, and various events along the way. This journal entry was recorded by Lewis and talks about his encounter with a bear.

Vocabulary Connection

Discuss unfamiliar vocabulary encountered in the text. Some possible words are listed below. After identifying the difficult words, discuss them within the context of the text.

- **descended**—climbed down
- **discharging**—to ooze out
- **perceived**—seen
- **recollected**—remembered
- **briskly**—quickly
- **conceal**—to hide
- **pitched**—to come at with force
- **obliged**—to have to, to be forced to
- **espontoon**—a weapon with a pointed end like a spear
- **precipitation**—haste or speed
- **retained**—kept
- **endeavored**—tried to figure out
- **talons**—claws
- **thwarted**—ruined

Extension Idea

- Have students imagine they are members of the Corps of Discovery. Tell them to choose a place on the trail. Are they traveling west or east? Have them write a journal entry that tells about a day at that spot on the trail with Lewis and Clark. What do they see, hear, smell, and taste? Allow students to share their entries with the class. If time allows, have students create their own reader's theater scripts based on their journal entries and let the class perform these reader's theaters.

Friday, June 14, 1805, Journal Entry

By Meriwether Lewis

I decended the hills and directed my course to the bend of the Missouri near which there was a herd of at least a thousand buffaloe; here I thought it would be well to kill a buffaloe and leave him untill my return from the river and if I then found that I had not time to get back to camp this evening to remain all night here there being a few sticks of drift wood lying along shore which would answer for my fire, and a few sattering cottonwood trees a few hundred yards below which would afford me at least a semblance of a shelter. under this impression I scelected a fat buffaloe and shot him very well, through the lungs; while I was gazeing attentively on the poor anamal discharging blood in streams from his mouth and nostrils, expecting him to fall every instant, and having entirely forgotton to reload my rifle, a large white, or reather brown bear, had perceived and crept on me within 20 steps before I discovered him; in the first moment I drew up my gun to shoot, but at the same instant recolected that she was not loaded and that he was too near for me to hope to perform this opperation before he reached me, as he was then briskly advancing on me; it was an open level plain, not a bush within miles nor a tree within less than three hundred yards of me; the river bank was sloping and not more than three feet above the level of the water; in short there was no place by means of which I could conceal myself from this monster untill I could charge my rifle; in this situation I thought of retreating in a brisk walk as fast as he was advancing untill I could reach a tree about 300 yards below me, but I had no sooner terned myself about but he pitched at me, open mouthed and full speed, I ran about 80 yards and found he gained on me fast, I then run into the water the idea struk me to get into the water to such debth that I could stand and he would be obliged to swim, and that I could in that situation defend myself with my espontoon; accordingly I ran haistily into the water about waist deep, and faced about and presented the point of my espontoon, at this instant he arrived at the edge of the water within about 20 feet of me; the moment I put myself in this attitude of defence he sudonly wheeled about as if frightened, declined the combat on such unequal grounds, and retreated with quite as great precipitation as he had just before pursued me. as soon as I saw him run off in that manner I returned to the shore and charged my gun, which I had still retained in my hand throughout this curious adventure. I saw him run through the level open plain about three miles, till he disappeared in the woods on medecine river; during the whole of this distance he ran at full speed, sometimes appearing to look behind him as if he expected pursuit. I now began to reflect on this novil occurrence and indeavoured to account for this sudden retreat of the bear. I at first thought that perhaps he had not smelt me before he arrived at the waters edge so near me, but I then reflected that he had pursued me for about 80 or 90 yards before I took the water and on examination saw the grownd toarn with his tallons immediately on the impression of my steps; and the cause of his allarm still remains with me misterious and unaccountable.— so it was and I feelt myself not a little gratifyed that he had declined the combat. My gun reloaded I felt confidence once more in my strength; and determined not to be thwarted in my design of visiting medicine river, but determined never again to suffer my peice to be longer empty than the time she necessarily required to charge her.

Name _____

Lewis and the Bear—Reader's Theater

R1:   I descended the hills and directed my course to the bend of the Missouri near which there was a herd of at least a thousand buffalo.

R2:   Here, I thought it would be well to kill a buffalo and leave him until my return from the river.

R3:   And, if I then found that I had not time to get back to camp this evening to remain all night here.

R4:   Under this impression, I selected a fat buffalo and shot him very well, through the lungs.

All: Bang!

R5:   While I was gazing attentively on the poor animal discharging blood in streams from his mouth and nostrils,

R1:   expecting him to fall every instant, and having entirely forgotten to reload my rifle,

R2:   a large white, or rather brown bear, had perceived and crept on me within 20 steps before I discovered him.

All: Oh no!

R3:   In the first moment, I drew up my gun to shoot, but at the same instant recollected that she was not loaded,

R4:   and that he was too near for me to hope to perform this operation before he reached me,

R5:   as he was then briskly advancing on me.

All: What should I do?

R1:   It was an open level plain, not a bush within miles nor a tree within less than 300 yards of me.

R2:   The riverbank was sloping and not more than three feet above the level of the water.

Lewis and the Bear—
Reader's Theater (cont.)

R3: In short, there was no place by means of which I could conceal myself from this monster until I could charge my rifle.

All: Help!

R4: I thought of retreating in a brisk walk as fast as he was advancing until I could reach a tree about 300 yards below me,

R5: but I had no sooner turned myself about but he pitched at me,

R1: open mouthed and full speed.

All: Ahhhh!

R2: I ran about 80 yards and found he gained on me fast,

R3: The idea struck me to get into the water to such depth that I could stand and he would be obliged to swim,

R4: In that situation, I could defend myself with my espontoon.

R5: Accordingly, I ran hastily into the water about waist deep, and faced about and presented the point of my espontoon.

All: Come and get me!

R1: At this instant, he arrived at the edge of the water within about 20 feet of me.

R2: The moment I put myself in this attitude of defense he suddenly wheeled about as if frightened,

R3: declined the combat on such unequal grounds,

R4: and retreated with quite as great precipitation as he had just before pursued me.

All: Ha, ha!

R5: As soon as I saw him run off in that manner I returned to the shore and charged my gun,

Lewis and the Bear— Reader's Theater *(cont.)*

R1:   which I had still retained in my hand throughout this curious adventure.

R2:   I saw him run through the level open plain about three miles, till he disappeared in the woods on Medicine River.

R3:   During the whole of this distance, he ran at full speed, sometimes appearing to look behind him as if he expected pursuit.

All: And stay away!

R4:   I now began to reflect on this novel occurrence and endeavored to account for this sudden retreat of the bear.

R5:   I at first thought that perhaps he had not smelt me before he arrived at the waters edge so near me,

R1:   but I then reflected that he had pursued me for about 80 or 90 yards before I took the water.

R2:   On examination, I saw the ground torn with his talons immediately on the impression of my steps.

R3:   The cause of his alarm still remains with me mysterious and unaccountable.

R4:   So, it was and I felt myself not a little gratified that he had declined the combat.

All: Whew!

R5:   My gun reloaded, I felt confidence once more in my strength,

R1:   and determined not to be thwarted in my design of visiting Medicine River.

R2:   But determined never again to suffer my piece to be longer empty than the time she necessarily required to charge her.

Clark and His Men

Objective

√ Students will read passages fluently and accurately within an oral reading activity, focusing on correct phrasing.

Preparation

- Copy *Thursday, June 20, 1805, Journal Entry* (page 113) for each student.
- Copy *Exploring Clark's Journal* (page 114) for the teacher and each student.

Fluency Suggestions and Activities

You may want to complete the history and vocabulary activities on the following page before starting this fluency activity. An understanding of the historical context and vocabulary will help students analyze and read the piece fluently.

Note: You might want to complete this fluency activity during the month of May to commemorate the beginning of the Lewis and Clark Expedition.

1. Begin the lesson by dividing the students into small groups. Provide each student with a copy of *Exploring Clark's Journal* (page 114). Instruct each group to discuss and answer only questions one through three. Then, gather the class together to discuss their responses to the questions.

2. Distribute copies of *Thursday, June 20, 1805, Journal Entry* (page 113) to students. For this activity, the text of Clark's journal entry has been edited. Rather than leaving the text with its multitude of spelling errors (common in Lewis and Clark's journals), they've been corrected to better allow students a chance to read the text fluently.

3. Read the journal entry aloud, modeling fluent reading. Read it again, and draw the students' attention to the phrasing used as you read. Read the first line in a choppy, word-by-word manner. Then read it fluently. Ask students to compare the two readings. Explain that proper phrasing makes readings easier to understand.

4. Have students complete the remainder of questions from *Exploring Clark's Journal* in their groups and then discuss the journal entry as a class.

5. Have students work in pairs to practice reading the journal entry, focusing on correct phrasing. When students have had the opportunity to practice reading the poem several times and on a few different occasions, have students recite this journal entry to various teachers in the building.

Clark and His Men (cont.)

History Connection

Introduce William Clark's journal entry using the information provided below.

William Clark knew Meriwether Lewis from his days in the army. Clark was an army officer and knew how to live in the wild. He was also outgoing, and this fit well with the quiet Lewis. Clark was talented at drawing maps and building things. Together, Lewis and Clark made a great team. The other men on the Corps had special talents too. Some were tailors, carpenters, and others were army men. Only one man died during the three years they were gone. They were an amazing team of men, and their trip changed America forever.

Vocabulary Connection

Discuss unfamiliar vocabulary encountered in the text. Some possible words are listed below. After identifying the difficult words, discuss them within the context of the text.

- **calculate**—to estimate or judge
- **sufficiently small**—small enough
- **dispatch**—to send
- **intended**—planned
- **hazard**—threaten
- **expedition**—a trip or voyage
- **scheme in contemplation**—thoughts about a plan
- **perish**—die
- **perilous**—dangerous
- **repining**—complaining
- **fortitude**—patiently bearing pain with courage

Extension Ideas

- Allow students to plan an expedition to a place they have never been. This should be somewhere near or in your community. It can be a new restaurant, store, or hiking trail. They should choose others to go with them (their family or friends). Have students go on this expedition and then write about their adventures. Provide time for students to share their adventures with the class.

- Have students think about what the trip was like for Lewis's dog, Seaman. Suppose he could keep a journal too. What would a day on the trail be like for him? Have students write a journal entry from his point of view.

Name _____

Thursday, June 20, 1805, Journal Entry

By William Clark

Not having seen the Snake Indians or knowing in fact whether to calculate on their friendship or hostility, we have conceived our party sufficiently small, and therefore have concluded not to dispatch a canoe with a part of our men to St. Louis as we have intended early in the spring.

We fear also that such a measure might also discourage those who would in such case remain, and might possibly hazard the fate of the expedition.

We have never hinted to any one of the party that we had such a scheme in contemplation, and all appear perfectly to have made up their minds to succeed in the expedition or perish in the attempt.

We all believe that we are about to enter on the most perilous and difficult part of our voyage, yet I see no one repining. All appear ready to meet those difficulties which await us with resolution and becoming fortitude.

Name _____

Exploring Clark's Journal

Directions: Before reading the journal entry, answer questions 1–3. After reading the journal entry, work with your group to answer questions 4–5.

1. William Clark had been an officer in the army before being asked to join the Corps of Discovery. Do you think he was afraid to go on this expedition?

   _____

   _____

   _____

2. How do you think Clark felt about having such an important friend as Meriwether Lewis, who was the secretary to the president of the United States?

   _____

   _____

   _____

3. What if Clark had approached you about joining the corps? Would you have wanted to serve under a leader like Clark? Explain your answer.

   _____

   _____

   _____

4. Does Clark sound scared about what lays ahead? Would you have been scared if you were Clark?

   _____

   _____

   _____

5. Imagine you are York, Clark's slave. On another sheet of paper, write a journal entry about going on this expedition.

Hailing the Chief

Objective

√ Students will deliver a class paired reading, oral presentations, performing a song for two voices fluently with changes in tone, voice, timing, and expression.

Preparation

- Make an overhead transparency of the song, "Hail to the Chief" (page 117).
- Copy *"Hail to the Chief"—A Song for Two Voices* (page 118) for each student.
- For optional use, copy *A Jingle for the New Chief* (page 119) for each student.

Fluency Suggestions and Activities

You may want to complete the history and vocabulary activities on the following page before starting this fluency activity. An understanding of the historical context and vocabulary will help students analyze and read the piece fluently.

Note: You may want to hold this presentation around the presidential inauguration day in January, just after school government elections, or when a new PTA president takes over.

1. Tell students that a mystery guest is coming to their class. To honor this guest, a special song has been chosen. Display the song, "Hail to the Chief" (page 117), on the overhead projector. Read it aloud for the students, modeling fluent reading. Ask students to offer their thoughts about what the words in this song mean. Find out if they know what kind of mystery guest will visit based on the words to the song. (Most of them might know that the words are referring to the president of the United States.) Tell students that the president of the PTA (or the student government president) will be visiting the classroom to hear their reading performance of this song. They will be reading this song as a class using two voices.

2. Read the script aloud together several times. Model reading lines with changes in pitch, tone, and timing to achieve different effects. Ask students to look for clues in the text that tell them how to read it (e.g., commas, periods, or exclamation points for emphasis).

3. Distribute *"Hail to the Chief"—A Song for Two Voices* (page 118). Draw their attention to the way the words are divided into parts for Voice 1 and Voice 2. Voice 1 begins the reading because the first line of the poem is below that heading. The next line falls under the heading Voice 2. Some lines of the poem are read together, as they fall below both headings in the same place. These lines are also indicated in bold text.

4. Invite two students to demonstrate reading of a few lines of the song for the class. Then, allow time for students to work in pairs to practice reading the song this way. They should make sure that both students get a chance to read each part.

5. Next, divide the class into the two groups. Assign each group one of the "voices" and practice reading the song as a class with two voices.

6. Arrange for the PTA president (or student government president) to visit the classroom to hear the class read the song. Then, if time allows, have students voice their opinions to this president on what they would like to see improved in the school.

Hailing the Chief (cont.)

History Connection

Discuss the song "Hail to the Chief" and the history behind it using the information below.

"Hail to the Chief" was first published in 1812 during President James Madison's term. It is believed that Walter Scott wrote the words and James Sanderson wrote the music. Interestingly enough, the words are rarely sung. The tune is what is familiar. The song was first played to announce a president during Martin Van Buren's inaugural ceremony in 1837. It is now the official presidential anthem, which is played at various events at the White House.

Vocabulary Connection

Discuss unfamiliar vocabulary encountered in the text. Some possible words are listed below. After identifying the difficult words, discuss them within the context of the text.

- **salute**—to greet by raising the right hand to the forehead

- **pledge**—to promise

- **cooperation**—the action of working together

- **noble**—having excellent qualities

Extension Ideas

- Have students listen to the music from "Hail to the Chief." Let them practice singing the song to this music. Then, have them work with partners to create different types of music and beats for the words of the song. They can practice singing the song and then present their creative songs to the class.

- If time permits, have the PTA/SGA president present problems having to do with the school to the class. The class can brainstorm ideas for fundraising, possible rules, or other ideas to make the school run smoother.

- Distribute copies of *A Jingle for the New Chief* (page 119) to the students. They will be adding another four lines to the song, "Hail to the Chief" for advertising purposes. These four lines should be to the same tune and advertise for new candidates for president. Allow students to present their songs to the class.

Hail to the Chief

By Sir Walter Scott

Hail to the Chief we have chosen for the nation,

Hail to the Chief! We salute him, one and all.

Hail to the Chief, as we pledge cooperation

In proud fulfillment of a great, noble call.

Yours is the aim to make this grand country grander,

This you will do, That's our strong, firm belief.

Hail to the one we selected as commander,

Hail to the President! Hail to the Chief!

Name _____

"Hail to the Chief"— A Song for Two Voices

Voice 1

Hail to the Chief

Hail to the Chief!

Hail to the Chief,

In proud fulfillment of a great, noble call.

Yours is the aim

This you will do,

Hail to the one

Hail to the President!
Hail to the Chief!

Voice 2

we have chosen for the nation,

We salute him, one and all.

as we pledge cooperation

In proud fulfillment of a great, noble call.

to make this grand country grander,

That's our strong, firm belief.

we selected as commander,

Hail to the President!
Hail to the Chief!

Name _____

A Jingle for the New Chief

Directions: The staff at the White House has put you in charge of finding candidates for the next election. You have decided to create an advertisement in the form of a song to be played on the radio. Write another eight lines to the same tune as "Hail to the Chief" in the space below. Remember, your advertisement should add at least another eight lines to the song, "Hail to the Chief."

_____

_____

_____

_____

_____

_____

_____

Mr. Madison's War

Objective

√ Students will deliver a class paired reading, oral presentations, performing a song for two voices fluently with changes in tone, voice, timing, and expression.

Preparation

- Make an overhead transparency of the song, "Ye Parliament of England" (page 122).
- Copy *"Ye Parliament of England"—A Song for Two Voices* (pages 123–124) for each student.
- For optional use, copy *The Ships in War* (page 125) for each student.

Fluency Suggestions and Activities

You may want to complete the history and vocabulary activities on the following page before starting this fluency activity. An understanding of the historical context and vocabulary will help students analyze and read the piece fluently.

Note: You might want to complete this activity during the month of February to remember the end of the War of 1812.

1. Place the transparency of the song, "Ye Parliament of England" (page 122), on the overhead and read it aloud for the students, modeling fluent reading. Ask them to offer their thoughts about what the song means.

2. Explain to the students that they will all have the opportunity to perform this poem in pairs. Arrange to have each pair of students perform this reading for a staff member in your school. (You could put up a sign-up sheet in the teachers' lounge and ask for teachers who are willing to have your students read for them.)

3. Distribute copies of *"Ye Parliament of England"—A Song for Two Voices* (pages 123–124) and draw student's attention to the layout of the words of the song. Explain that the song is divided into parts for Voice 1 and Voice 2. Voice 1 begins the reading because the first line of the song is below that heading. The next line is under the heading Voice 2. Some lines of the song are read together. These lines are bolded.

4. Encourage students to focus on voice tone, timing, and facial expressions as they read. Discuss with students how their tone of voice can affect the mood of the song. Discuss how the speed at which they read is important, as well. Emphasize to the students that since they are performing this reading, it is important to think about their facial expressions because someone will be watching them perform.

5. Invite two students to model reading a few lines of the song for the class. Tell the students that this kind of song takes practice to read fluently. Divide the students into pairs and tell them that they will be performing this piece for a staff member in the school.

6. Allow the students time to practice their parts. They should practice their parts in the classroom on the day of the presentations, too.

Mr. Madison's War (cont.)

History Connection

Introduce "Ye Parliament of England" using the information provided below.

The beginning of the 1800s brought about some trouble for the new country. British and French ships began to stop American ships on the open seas. They wanted to control shipping and the new Americans were infringing on their business. James Madison became the fourth president of the United States in 1809. He hoped to avoid war, but the insults to his nation became too much to bear. Congress declared war in 1812. At first, things did not go well for the Americans. Many people were angry with President Madison and called it "Mr. Madison's War." During the war America built many ships and after some time began sinking the British ships. America stood up to the big nation of Great Britain and won back the respect they felt they deserved. The war lasted until 1814 when both sides signed a treaty. This song is to the tune of "The War of 1812," but it is written from the American point of view.

Vocabulary Connection

Discuss unfamiliar vocabulary encountered in the text. Some possible words are listed below. After identifying the difficult words, discuss them within the context of the text.

- **Parliament**—governing body of Great Britain
- **rue**—regret
- **shant**—shall not
- **impressed**—forced to join the military
- **frigates**—medium-sized warships
- **annoy**—to bother

Extension Ideas

- Have students perform a class singing of this song for another class in the school or for the entire office staff.
- Have students pick out the names of ships mentioned in the song. Then distribute *The Ships in War* (page 125) to the students. Let students choose one ship from the list and find out more about it while working with a partner. Each pair of students can present their information on an overhead and teach a small lesson about that ship and what happened to it in the War of 1812.

Ye Parliament of England

Ye Parliament of England,
You Lords and commons, too,
Consider well what you're about
And what you're going to do.
You're now to fight with Yankees,
I'm sure you'll rue the day,
You roused the Sons of Liberty
In North America.

You first confined our commerce,
And said our ships shant trade,
You next impressed our seamen,
And used them as your slaves;
You then insulted Rodgers,
While ploughing o'er the main,
And had we not declared war,
You'd have done it o'er again.

You thought our frigates were but few,
And Yankees would not fight,
Until brave *Hull* your *Guerriere* took,
And banished her from your sight.
The *Wasp* then took your *Frolic*,
We'll nothing say to that,
The *Poictiers* being of the line,
Of course she took her back.

Then next, upon Lake Erie,
Where Perry had some fun,
Your own he beat your naval force,
And caused them for to run;
This was to you a sore defeat,
The like ne'er known before,
Your British Squadron beat complete
Some took, some run ashore.

There's Rodgers, in the *President*,
Will burn, sink, and destroy;
The *Congress*, on the Brazil coast,
Your commerce will annoy;
The *Essex*, in the South Seas,
Will put out all your lights,
The flag she waves at her mast-head:
"Free Trade and Sailors' Rights!"

Lament, ye sons of Britain,
Far distant is the day
When you'll regain by British force
What you're lost in America;
Go tell your King and parliament,
By all the world 'tis known,
That British force, by sea and land,
By Yankees is o'erthrown.

Use every endeavor,
And strive to make a peace,
For Yankee ships are building fast,
Their Navy to increase;
They will enforce their commerce,
The laws by Heaven were made,
That Yankee ships in time of peace,
To any port may trade.

Name _____

"Ye Parliament of England"— A Song for Two Voices

Voice 1

Ye Parliament of England,

Consider well what you're about

You're now to fight with Yankees,

**You roused the Sons of Liberty
in North America.**

You first confined our commerce,

You next impressed our seamen,

You then insulted Rodgers,

**And had we not declared war,
You'd have done it o'er again.**

You thought our frigates were but few,

Until brave *Hull* your *Guerriere* took,

The *Wasp* then took your *Frolic*,

**The *Poictiers* being of the line,
Of course she took her back.**

Then next, upon Lake Erie,

Your own he beat your naval force,

This was to you a sore defeat,

Voice 2

You Lords and commons, too,

And what you're going to do.

I'm sure you'll rue the day,

**You roused the Sons of Liberty
in North America**

And said our ships can't trade,

And used them as your slaves;

While ploughing over the main,

**And had we not declared war,
You'd have done it o'er again.**

And Yankees would not fight,

And banished her from your sight.

We'll nothing say to that,

**The *Poictiers* being of the line,
Of course she took her back.**

Where Perry had some fun,

And caused them for to run;

The like never known before,

Ye Parliament of England— A Song for Two Voices *(cont.)*

Voice 1

Your British Squadron beat complete some took, some run ashore.

There's Rodgers, in the *President*,

The *Congress*, on the Brazil coast,

The *Essex*, in the South Seas,

The flag she waves at her mast-head: "Free Trade and Sailors' Rights!"

Lament, ye sons of Britain,

When you'll regain by British force

Go tell your King and parliament,

That British force, by sea and land, by Yankees is overthrown.

Use every endeavor,

For Yankee ships are building fast,

They will enforce their commerce,

That Yankee ships in time of peace, To any port may trade.

Voice 2

Your British Squadron beat complete some took, some run ashore.

Will burn, sink, and destroy;

Your commerce will annoy;

Will put out all your lights,

The flag she waves at her mast-head: "Free Trade and Sailors' Rights!"

Far distant is the day

What you're lost in America;

By all the world 'tis known,

That British force, by sea and land, by Yankees is overthrown.

And strive to make a peace,

Their Navy to increase;

The laws by Heaven were made,

That Yankee ships in time of peace, To any port may trade.

Name _____

The Ships in War

Directions: In the song, "Ye Parliament of England," there are many ships mentioned. Find out the information on one of these ships and present a mini-lesson to your class. Consult books, encyclopedias, and the Internet for your information. Use the template in the space below to help you organize your information. The list of ships includes the *Hull, Guerriere, Wasp, Frolic, Poictiers, Macedonian, President, Congress,* and *Essex.* Other ships you can research include: *Java, Peacock, Boxer,* and *Enterprising.*

Name of ship:
Year built:
Type of ship:
Major events:
Connection to the War of 1812:
How I will present my lesson:

Little House Books

Objective

√ Students will practice divided reading of the text in preparation for a performance in various classrooms.

Preparation

- Copy the *Fluency Assessment* (page 128) for each student.
- Gather various Laura Ingalls Wilder books (enough for one per student).
- Locate a tape recorder and audiotapes.

Fluency Suggestions and Activities

You may want to complete the history and vocabulary activities on the following page before starting this fluency activity. An understanding of the historical context and vocabulary will help students analyze and read the piece fluently.

Note: If possible have students complete this activity to celebrate Laura Ingalls Wilder's birthday on February 7.

1. Begin by reading a selection from one of the *Little House* books written by Laura Ingalls Wilder. Read the selection aloud, modeling fluent reading. Ask students if they have ever read any of her books.

2. Have students think about what life was like for Laura Ingalls as a pioneer girl. Allow them to write their ideas down. Then, have students share their ideas with the entire class. Next, provide copies of various Laura Ingalls Wilder books for students to look through. Students will then be able to read about some of the adventures that a pioneer girl faced.

3. Tell each student to choose a section of his or her book that is interesting to them. The parts that they choose should describe some adventure that Laura had or something about what it was like to live during that time. Explain that they will be reading this chapter throughout the week for a younger class in the school. Check their selections to ensure that they have chosen good sections for whatever class they will be visiting. They need to break the selection into five sections to be read, one per day. Some students might need some guidance on how to divide their chosen selection into good parts.

4. After students have shown you their chosen selections, allow them time to practice reading them aloud. Have each student create one tape recording of the reading. Then, distribute copies of the *Fluency Assessment* (page 128) for students to use to evaluate their fluency on the recordings. Remind the students to think about how to use their voices to make the reading selection interesting. Allow the students several days in class to practice the reading of their selections.

5. Arrange ahead of time for each student to visit a classroom every day during the week to read his or her selection. One selection will be read on Monday, the next selection from will be read on Tuesday, and so on.

Little House Books (cont.)

History Connection

Introduce Laura Ingalls Wilder's books using the information provided below.

Laura Ingalls was born on February 7, 1867, in Wisconsin. Her parents were farmers who moved out west to take advantage of the Homestead Act, an agreement from the government that gave farmers five years to work the land and make it better in return for ownership of the farm. Laura's family lived in log cabins and sod houses. Her family suffered through blizzards, ruined crops, and hunger. She became a teacher when she was only 15 years old. Later, she became a writer of children's books about life as a pioneer. Her books have been read for many years by children and adults alike.

Vocabulary Connection

Discuss unfamiliar vocabulary encountered in the text. Some possible words are listed below. After identifying the difficult words, discuss them within the context of the text.

- **sod houses**—homes made out of thick grass and mud

- **pioneer**—someone who went out to the unsettled western land to create a new life

- **Homestead Act**—the act signed by Abraham Lincoln that allowed a farmer to own the land if he had lived on the land and farmed it for five years

Extension Ideas

- If possible, allow students to watch an episode of the "Little House on the Prairie" television show. Students can write a short story as if they were Laura Ingalls Wilder based on that television show. Then, students can compare their stories with stories in her books to see how they are similar.

- Allow students to explore the Internet to find out more about Laura Ingalls Wilder. They can print out maps showing the different places that Laura lived and look at primary source documents that tell about the Homestead Act.

Name_____

Fluency Assessment

Directions: Listen to the recording of your voice, and then answer the following questions.

1. What do you like about the way you read?

   _____

   _____

2. What don't you like about the way you read?

   _____

   _____

3. Was the reading too fast, too slow, or just right?

   _____

4. Did you stumble on any words? Explain.

   _____

   _____

5. Which words or phrases did you emphasize in the reading and why did you choose to emphasize them?

   _____

   _____

   _____

   _____

6. On the lines below, write your plan for improving your fluency in preparation for your presentation to another class.

   _____

   _____

   _____

   _____

   _____

   _____

Pioneer Girl

Objective

√ Students will participate in cooperative learning and improve expressive reading skills by engaging in reader's theater.

Preparation

- Copy *Little House in the Big Woods—Reader's Theater* (pages 131–132) for each student.
- Provide copies of *Little House* books, one for each student.
- Copy *Reader's Theater for Laura Ingalls Wilder* (page 133) for each student.
- Provide highlighters.

Fluency Suggestions and Activities

You may want to complete the history activity on the following page before starting this fluency activity. An understanding of the historical context will help students analyze and read the piece fluently.

1. Obtain a copy of *Little House in the Big Woods* by Laura Ingalls Wilder. Begin by reading the first half of the first chapter to your students.

2. Distribute copies of *Little House in the Big Woods—Reader's Theater* (pages 131–132) and read through it once, modeling fluent reading. Point out that this reader's theater script is about the passage that you just read in the book.

3. Read the script together several times. Model reading lines with changes in pitch, tone, and timing to achieve different effects. Ask students to look for clues in the text that tell them how to read it (e.g., commas or exclamation points).

4. Place students into groups of three. Allow students time to read through the script several times. Have the groups perform their readings for the class.

5. Then, tell students that they will be working in groups to write and perform their own reader's theater scripts. This time, place students in groups of four. You can assign a section of a book to groups or allow each group to choose its own section from one of Laura Ingalls Wilder's books to create their reader's theater. Distribute copies of *Reader's Theater for Laura Ingalls Wilder* (page 133) to the students.

6. When students finish writing their reader's theater scripts, allow time for them to practice performing them. Have students create invitations and give them to their parents a week before the performance. Students can perform their reader's theater scripts for those parent visitors.

Pioneer Girl (cont.)

History Connection

Introduce *Little House in the Big Woods* using the information provided below.

When Laura Ingalls was 18, she married Almanzo Wilder. He was a farmer. A year later, they had a baby girl named Rose. The three of them lived as pioneers struggling through fires, droughts, illnesses, and debt. When Almanzo became ill, the family moved to Rocky Ridge Farm in Mansfield, Missouri. Laura was over 60 years old when she wrote her first book called *Pioneer Girl*. She then edited this book and got it published under the title, *Little House in the Big Woods*. She proceeded to write other children's books about life as a pioneer. Her books became best sellers and people from all around began to visit the places that she lived, including her house at Rocky Ridge Farm. Today, there are museums in the towns where she lived to honor this amazing woman.

Extension Ideas

- Laura Ingalls Wilder kept a detailed journal about her travels and daily life. Have students write a journal entry about one day in Wilder's life. Challenge students to think about the following questions: What kinds of chores did she do during the day? What did her family do for entertainment?

- Have students think about the changes that Laura Ingalls Wilder experienced during her 90 years of life. She rode in covered wagons, trains, cars, and even airplanes. She died in 1957. What if she were alive today? What would she think of all the new technology? Have students compose a letter from her telling her feelings about the changes in today's society.

Name _____

Little House in the Big Woods— Reader's Theater

R1: A long time ago, a little girl by the name of Laura lived in the Big Woods of Wisconsin.

R2: They lived in a little gray house made from logs.

R3: As far as they could see there were

All: **trees, trees, and more trees!**

R1: No one lived nearby.

R2: Just animals like bears, wild cats, and foxes had their homes in the area.

R3: Laura lived with her ma and pa

R1: and her two sisters, Carrie and Mary.

R2: At night, Laura would listen to the sounds all around her.

R3: The trees whispered,

All: **sssssssss!**

R1: the wolf howled,

All: **awooooo!**

R2: and her dog Jack growled a deep growl.

All: **Rrrrrr!**

R3: One night, Laura heard their pig squealing wildly.

R1: She ran to the window to see what was the matter.

Little House in the Big Woods— Reader's Theater *(cont.)*

R2:   Her father had already jumped out of bed,

R3:   grabbed his gun,

R1:   and made his way to the pigpen.

R2:   In the darkness, Pa had seen the shape of a big black bear

R3:   hovering over the pigpen.

R1:   The bear lifted its claw and let out a huge growl

All: **Grrrr!**

R2:   Pa shivered in his boots.

R3:   Just as the bear reached inside the pen to snatch up the pig

R1:   Pa hastily took his gun and fired at the bear.

R2:   He missed the bear, but luckily the gunshot scared the bear away

R3:   and the pig was safe.

R1:   Laura was disappointed that Pa did not kill the bear

R2:   because she loved bear meat.

R3:   But Pa said,

All: **"Well at least I saved the bacon!"**

Name_____

Reader's Theater for Laura Ingalls Wilder

Directions: Write your own reader's theater script for a story by Laura Ingalls Wilder in the space below. Be sure to identify the reader (R1, R2, R3, or R4) Also, be sure to determine lines that will be read by "All." You may want to use a highlighter to draw attention to the lines read by all students in your group.

Title of book: _____

Chapter and pages: _____

Title of reader's theater: _____

Script: _____

_____

_____

_____

_____

_____

_____

_____

_____

_____

_____

_____

_____

A Song for Harriet

Objective

√ Students will deliver a group oral presentation and read passages fluently with changes in tone, voice, timing, and expression.

Preparation

- Copy the song, "Follow the Drinking Gourd" (page 136), for the teacher and each student.
- Copy *"Follow the Drinking Gourd"—Echo Reading* (page 137) for each student.
- Make an overhead transparency of *The Underground Railroad Map* (page 138).
- For optional use, copy *Coded Words* (page 139) for each student.
- Provide highlighters.

Fluency Suggestions and Activities

You may want to complete the history and vocabulary activities on the following page before starting this fluency activity. An understanding of the historical context and vocabulary will help students analyze and read the piece fluently.

Note: You may want to have this presentation near the time of Vernal Equinox in March since the song refers to the time when the sun is getting higher in the sky at noon. It also ties in with a study on astronomy.

1. Begin by placing a transparency of *The Underground Railroad Map* (page 138) on the overhead projector. Explain to students that these are the routes that slaves took to freedom. Today, we have maps of this, but back then they did not have maps and many of them could not read. Instead, they received directions through songs.

2. Give each student a copy of the song, "Follow the Drinking Gourd" (page 136). Read the song aloud, modeling fluent reading. If possible, have students listen to a recording of the song after your reading. Tell students that they will be making their own recording by reciting the words of the song.

3. Read the poem as an echo reading with the class. You read two lines and the students read them back to you. Continue until you have read the entire poem. Ask students to look for clues in the text that tell them how to read it (e.g., commas, exclamation marks, periods, or repetition).

4. Place the students in groups of four. Each group will be responsible for presenting an echo reading on audiotape. Explain that these tapes will be placed in rooms throughout the school for younger students to hear. Along with the tape, provide copies of the text so that other students can read along with the tape, echoing the various parts.

5. Once the students are in their groups, give them copies of *"Follow the Drinking Gourd"— Echo Reading* (page 137). This sheet has the piece broken into echo reading parts for four students. Any groups that have more than or fewer than four students will need to alter their assignment so that every student participates (e.g., two students read together, students read fewer lines, or students read more lines).

6. On the day of the recordings, tape-record each group's performance on an audiotape. Remind students to use their voices to convey the message of the song.

A Song for Harriet *(cont.)*

History Connection

Introduce "Follow the Drinking Gourd" using the information provided below.

During the time of slavery in the United States, some slaves tried to escape to the North to gain their freedom. Slave owners knew this, so they tried to keep their slaves ignorant about the geography of the area. They also didn't want their slaves learning which direction was north. Many slaves knew that Polaris, the North Star, would guide them north, but the terrain was sometimes dangerous. In 1831, members of the Underground Railroad began traveling south to teach routes to slaves who wanted to escape. Slaves were taught at a very young age how to find the Big Dipper in the sky. They referred to the Big Dipper in the sky as a drinking gourd. "Follow the Drinking Gourd" was a song that gave directions from Alabama and Mississippi to the North where slaves could gain their freedom. An old man named Peg Leg Joe went from plantation to plantation teaching slaves this song so that they would know how to escape.

Vocabulary Connection

Discuss unfamiliar vocabulary encountered in the text. Some possible words are listed below. After identifying the difficult words, discuss them within the context of the text.

- **drinking gourd**—a dipper used for liquids; the Big Dipper in the sky
- **awaiting**—waiting
- **quail**—a type of bird that migrates to the South
- **peg**—a leg made from wood

Extension Ideas

- Have students study a map of the sun's movement throughout the year. This type of map can be found on the Internet. Then, have them track the sun for a week, noting the time that the sun rises and sets every day.

- Show students a diagram of the Big Dipper and the Little Dipper. Assign them to find both of these on a clear night by first locating the North Star.

- Discuss the Underground Railroad. Then, distribute copies of *Coded Words* (page 139) to students. Have students complete the activities on this page relating to the song "Follow the Drinking Gourd."

Follow the Drinking Gourd

Follow the drinking gourd!
Follow the drinking gourd.
For the old man is awaiting for to carry you to freedom
If you follow the drinking gourd.

When the sun comes back and the first quail calls,
Follow the drinking gourd,
For the old man is awaiting for to carry you to freedom
If you follow the drinking gourd.

The riverbank makes a very good road,
The dead trees will show you the way,
Left foot, peg foot traveling on,
Following the drinking gourd.

The river ends between two hills,
Follow the drinking gourd,
There's another river on the other side,
Follow the drinking gourd.

Where the great big river meets the little river,
Follow the drinking gourd,
The old man is awaiting for to carry you to freedom
If you follow the drinking gourd.

Name _____

"Follow the Drinking Gourd"— Echo Reading

All
Follow the drinking gourd!
Follow the drinking gourd.
For the old man is awaiting for to
    carry you to freedom
If you follow the drinking gourd.

Student 1
When the sun comes back and the first
    quail calls,
Follow the drinking gourd,
(Audience echoes)

Student 2
For the old man is awaiting for to carry
    you to freedom
If you follow the drinking gourd.
(Audience echoes)

All
Follow the drinking gourd!
Follow the drinking gourd.
For the old man is awaiting for to
    carry you to freedom
If you follow the drinking gourd.

Student 3
The riverbank makes a very good road,
The dead trees will show you the way,
(Audience echoes)

Student 4
Left foot, peg foot traveling on,
Following the drinking gourd.
(Audience echoes)

All
Follow the drinking gourd!
Follow the drinking gourd.
For the old man is awaiting for to
    carry you to freedom
If you follow the drinking gourd.

Student 1
The river ends between two hills,
Follow the drinking gourd,
(Audience echoes)

Student 2
There's another river on the other side,
Follow the drinking gourd.
(Audience echoes)

All
Follow the drinking gourd!
Follow the drinking gourd.
For the old man is awaiting for to
    carry you to freedom
If you follow the drinking gourd.

Student 3
Where the great big river meets the
    little river,
Follow the drinking gourd,
(Audience echoes)

Student 4
The old man is awaiting for to carry you
    to freedom
If you follow the drinking gourd.
(Audience echoes)

All
Follow the drinking gourd!
Follow the drinking gourd.
For the old man is awaiting for to
    carry you to freedom
If you follow the drinking gourd.

Underground Railroad Map

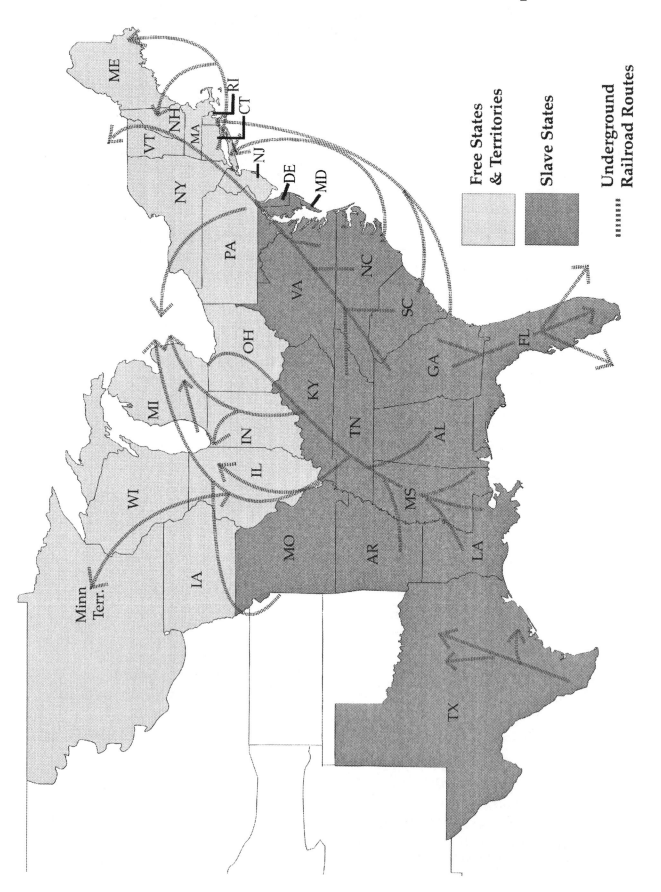

Name_____

Coded Words

Directions: Below are listed many of the coded words and phrases used by "conductors" when helping a slave escape along the Underground Railroad. After reading this list, highlight the ones that are found in the song, "Follow the Drinking Gourd." Then add three more original coded words or phrases to this list.

baggage—escaping slaves

bundles of wood—fugitives to be expected

Canaan—Canada

drinking gourd—Big Dipper and the North star

forwarding—taking fugitive slaves from station to station

Freedom Train—The Underground Railroad

Gospel Train—The Underground Railroad

Heaven or promised land—Canada

load of potatoes—escaping slaves hidden under the farm produce in a wagon

Moses—Harriet Tubman

parcel—fugitives to be expected

preachers—leaders, speakers about the Underground Railroad

River Jordan—Mississippi River

shepherds—people escorting slaves

station—place of safety and temporary refuge, safe house

station master—keeper of safe house

stockholder—donor of money, clothing, or food to the Underground Railroad

"The wind blows from the South today"—A warning to Underground Railroad workers that fugitive slaves were in the area

"When the sun comes back and the first quail calls"—A particular time of year good for escaping (early spring)

"The river bank makes a mighty good road"—A reminder that the tracking dogs can't follow the scent through the water

"The dead trees will show you the way"—A reminder that moss grows on the north side of dead trees (just in case the stars aren't visible)

"Left foot, peg foot"—A visual clue for escapees left by an Underground Railroad worker famous because of his wooden leg

"The river ends between two hills"—A clue for the directions to the Ohio River

"A friend with friends"—A password used to signal arrival of fugitives with an Underground Railroad conductor

"The friend of a friend sent me"—a password used by fugitives traveling alone to indicate they were sent by the Underground Railroad network

"Steal away, steal away, steal away to Jesus"—words to a song used to alert other slaves that an escape attempt was coming up

The Underground Railroad

Objective

√ Students will participate in cooperative learning and improve expressive reading skills by engaging in reader's theater.

Preparation

- Copy the song, "The Underground Railcar" (page 142), for the teacher.
- Copy *"The Underground Railcar"—Reader's Theater* (pages 143–144) for each student.
- Provide highlighters.

Fluency Suggestions and Activities

You may want to complete the history and vocabulary activities on the following page before starting this fluency activity. An understanding of the historical context and vocabulary will help students analyze and read the piece fluently.

Note: You might want to have students perform this reader's theater during a study on slavery in America or during Black History Month.

1. Model a fluent reading of the song, "The Underground Railcar" (page 142), for the students. Tell students that they will be performing this reading for some members of the local newspaper. If there is a small town newspaper in your community, contact them. Otherwise, contact the closest city newspaper and ask to speak to the person in charge of educational news. Have students send an invitation to this person. Invite other newspaper staff if possible.

2. Give each student a copy of *"The Underground Railcar"—Reader's Theater* (pages 143–144). Read the script together several times. Model reading lines with changes in pitch, tone, and timing to achieve different effects. Ask students to look for clues in the text that tell them how to read it.

3. Then, place students into groups of five. Assign parts to students by having them volunteer or audition. Have students highlight their parts. Or the entire class can participate in the presentation by altering the reading parts to suit the number of students in your classroom.

4. Have students read their assigned parts aloud in their groups. Provide time for practice individually and in small groups.

5. On the day of the performance, have students bring snacks for a small reception for the guests. Students can also share what they know about the Underground Railroad.

The Underground Railroad (cont.)

History Connection

Introduce "The Underground Railcar" using the information provided below.

"The Underground Railcar" was written and published in 1854 by George N. Allen. The term Underground Railroad was first used in the 1840s. Those who were trying to escape were called passengers and those trying to help others escape were called conductors. The brutal work and living conditions of slavery caused many slaves to risk their lives to find freedom along this trail. If slaves were caught, they were returned to their owners in chains and may have been beaten or killed. Harriet Tubman was called Moses because she helped slaves escape from their owners by guiding them along the Underground Railroad. "The Underground Railcar" is a song about the escape of a slave from the hands of his master to the free "shores" of Canada. The Underground Railroad carries him to freedom.

Vocabulary Connection

Discuss unfamiliar vocabulary encountered in the text. Some possible words are listed below. After identifying the difficult words, discuss them within the context of the text.

- **freeman**—a slave who has been set free
- **resolved**—decided
- **shun**—to push away
- **abhor'd**—abhorred; hated
- **fetters**—chains or shackles
- **embark**—to begin, to leave
- **yonder**—faraway
- **vain**—hopeless
- **stealing**—sneaking out of
- **haste**—hurry

Extension Idea

- Have students look at the words of the Emancipation Proclamation and rewrite them in their own words. Then, tell students to imagine they were slaves when Abraham Lincoln issued this proclamation. How would this make them feel? What could they do if they lived in a Border State since the proclamation did not apply to slaves there? Have them write letters to Abraham Lincoln telling him their feelings on this issue.

The Underground Railcar

By George N. Allen

I'm on my way to Canada a freeman's rights to share.
The cruel wrongs of Slavery I can no longer bear;
My heart is crush'd within me so while I remain a slave,
That I'm resolved to strike the blow for Freedom or the Grave!
O Great Father! do thou pity me.
And help me on to Canada where the panting slave is free!

I've served my Master all my days without the least reward,
And now I'm forc'd to flee away to shun the lash abhor'd;
The hounds are baying on my track, my Master's just behind,
Resolv'd that he will bring be back and fast his fetters bind.
O Great Father! do thou pity me.
And help me on to Canada where the panting slave is free!

I've heard that Queen Victoria has pledged us all a home
Beyond the reach of Slavery, if we will only come;
So I have fled this weary way, my guide the bright north star,
And now, thank God, I speed today in the Underground Railcar.
O old Master! why come after me,
I'm whizzing fast to Canada where the panting slave is free!

I now embark for yonder shore, sweet land of liberty.
The vessel soon will bear me o'er, and I shall then be free;
No more I'll dread the auctioneer, nor fear the Master's frowns,
No more I'll tremble lest I hear the baying of the hounds.
O old Master, 'tis vain to follow me.
I'm just in sight of Canada, where the panting slave is free!

Yes! I am safe in Canada—my soul and body free.
My blood and tears no more shall drench thy soil, O Tennessee!
Yet how can I suppress the tear that's stealing from my eye,
To think my friends and kindred dear as slaves must live and die.
O dear friends, haste and follow me,
For I am safe in Canada, where the panting slave is free!

Name _____

"The Underground Railcar"— Reader's Theater

R1: It is the 1850s, and you work six days a week on a plantation.

R2: Work, work, work! That is all you know. You are a slave who is owned by another human.

R3: Freedom? Did someone say freedom? What is that?

R4: I never thought I would know. I've heard whispers of others who have attempted to escape.

R5: It excites the blood in my body, and I know I have to take the chance.

R1: All of a sudden I'm on my way to Canada a freeman's rights to share.

R2: The cruel wrongs of Slavery I can no longer bear.

R3: My heart is crushed within me so while I remain a slave,

R4: That I'm resolved to strike the blow for Freedom or the Grave!

All: **O Great Father! do thou pity me
And help me on to Canada where the panting slave is free!**

R5: I've served my Master all my days without the least reward.

R1: And now I'm forced to flee away to shun the lash abhorred.

R2: The hounds are baying on my track, my Master's just behind,

R3: Resolved that he will bring me back and fast his fetters bind.

All: **O Great Father!
Do thou pity me and help me on to Canada where the panting slave is free!**

"The Underground Railcar"— Reader's Theater *(cont.)*

R4:   I've heard that Queen Victoria has pledged us all a home

R5:   Beyond the reach of Slavery, if we will only come.

R1:   So I have fled this weary way, my guide the bright north star.

R2:   And now, thank God, I speed today in the Underground Railcar.

All: **O old Master! Why come after me?**
            I'm whizzing fast to Canada where the panting slave is free!

R3:   I now embark for yonder shore, sweet land of liberty.

R4:   The vessel soon will bear me over, and I shall then be free.

R5:   No more I'll dread the auctioneer, nor fear the Master's frowns.

R1:   No more I'll tremble lest I hear the baying of the hounds.

All: **O old Master, it is vain to follow me.**
            I'm just in sight of Canada, where the panting slave is free!

R2:   Yes! I am safe in Canada—my soul and body free.

R3:   My blood and tears no more shall drench thy soil, O Tennessee!

R4:   Yet how can I suppress the tear that's stealing from my eye.

R5:   To think my friends and kindred dear as slaves must live and die.

All: **O dear friends, haste and follow me.**
            For I am safe in Canada, where the panting slave is free!

Sitting Bull Speaks His Mind

Objective

√ Students will read passages fluently and accurately within a cumulative choral-reading activity, focusing on correct conversational and expressive language.

Preparation

- Make an overhead transparency of *Sitting Bull to the Senate Committee* (page 147).
- Copy *Sitting Bull to the Senate Committee—Cumulative Choral Reading* (page 148) for each student.
- For optional use, copy *Sitting Bull Song* (page 149) for each student.

Fluency Suggestions and Activities

You may want to complete the history activity on the following page before starting this fluency activity. An understanding of the historical context will help students analyze and read the piece fluently.

Note: You might want to have students perform this reading at the end of the school year, which is near the anniversary of the Battle of Little Bighorn on June 25, 1876.

1. Place a transparency copy of *Sitting Bull to the Senate Committee* (page 147) on the overhead. Read it aloud, modeling fluent reading. Tell students that they will be reading this statement for a group of students in the school. If your school has a closed-captioned television circuit that broadcasts throughout the school, arrange for the class to perform it for the camera. Otherwise, video tape their performance and allow other classes to view the tape.

2. Distribute copies of *Sitting Bull to the Senate Committee—Cumulative Choral Reading* (page 148) to students. Read through the statement slowly, as a choral reading with the entire class. After each sentence, stop and look for clues in the text that tell you how to read it (e.g., commas, exclamation marks, period, or quotation marks).

3. Then, explain what a backwards cumulative choral reading is to the class. Tell students that everyone will begin reading Sitting Bull's statement. Then after one line, one student will stop reading. This process will continue until only one student is left reading.

4. To begin, you will need to assign parts to the students and give them a chance to practice. There are enough lines in the speech to accommodate 20 readers. So, depending on how many students you have, you will need to assign one or two students to every line. It is suggested that you assign your stronger readers to the lower numbers because they will have to read more of the poem.

5. Give students plenty of time to practice their parts before the day of their final performance.

Sitting Bull Speaks His Mind (cont.)

History Connection

Introduce Sitting Bull's speech using the information provided below.

Sitting Bull was a American Indian chief and a fierce warrior. As Sitting Bull saw more and more white men coming to the Black Hills, he and his people became angry. Gold had been discovered, and all of a sudden many white men came to the area hoping to get rich. Sitting Bull did not want his people to give up their way of life. The U.S. government tried to get him to sign treaties, but he refused to sign them. He believed these treaties would take away his people's freedom to roam their land. The government sent their army to control the Indians, but the army was slaughtered at the Battle of Little Bighorn in 1876. Sitting Bull then took his people to Canada to escape more soldiers. In Canada, the Indians began to starve. The Lakota Indians were forced to return and surrender. After spending two years in jail, Sitting Bull went to live on Standing Rock Reservation. Sitting Bull made this statement to a senate committee in what is now North Dakota in 1883.

Extension Idea

- Distribute copies of the *Sitting Bull Song* (page 149) to the students. Talk about the impact the music has on the meaning of the song. Have students list several ideas of music on the board before beginning the activity. They will be taking a song written for Sitting Bull and adding music to it. Then, they will sing it for their classmates.

Sitting Bull To the Senate Committee

By Sitting Bull

And yet you men have come here to talk with us, and you do not know who I am. If the Great Spirit has chosen any one to be the chief of this country it is myself. You have conducted yourself like men who have been drinking whiskey, and I came here to give you some advice. I have always been a chief, and have been made chief of all the land. Thirty-two years ago I was present at the [Fort Rice] council with the white man. Since then a great many questions have been asked me about it, and I always said, "Wait." Then the Black Hills council was held, and they asked me to give up that land, and I said, "Wait." I remember well all the promises that were made about that land . . . . You white men advise us to follow your ways, and therefore I talk as I do. When you have a piece of land, and anything trespasses on it, you catch and keep it until you get damages, and I am doing the same thing now. And I want you to tell this to the Great Father for me. I am looking into the future for the benefit of my children, and I want my country taken care of for me.

To the Senate Committee,
Standing Rock Agency, August 1883

Name _____

Sitting Bull to the Senate Committee— Cumulative Choral Reading

Line 20:   And yet you men have come here to talk with us,

Line 19:   and you do not know who I am.

Line 18:   If the Great Spirit has chosen anyone to be the chief of this country, it is myself.

Line 17:   You have conducted yourself like men who have been drinking whiskey,

Line 16:   and I came here to give you some advice.

Line 15:   I have always been a chief,

Line 14:   and have been made chief of all the land.

Line 13:   Thirty-two years ago I was present at the council with the white man.

Line 12:   Since then a great many questions have been asked me about it,

Line 11:   and I always said, "Wait."

Line 10:   Then the Black Hills council was held,

Line 9:   and they asked me to give up that land, and I said, "Wait."

Line 8:   I remember well all the promises that were made about that land.

Line 7:   You white men advise us to follow your ways, and therefore I talk as I do.

Line 6:   When you have a piece of land, and anything trespasses on it,

Line 5:   you catch and keep it until you get damages,

Line 4:   and I am doing the same thing now.

Line 3:   And I want you to tell this to the Great Father for me.

Line 2:   I am looking into the future for the benefit of my children,

Line 1:   and I want my country taken care of for me.

Name _____

Sitting Bull Song

By Stanley Vestal

> My father has given me this nation,
>
> In protecting them I have a hard time.
>
> No chance for me to live, Mother,
>
> You might as well mourn.

Directions: Use these lyrics to a song written about Sitting Bull to complete this assignment.

1. Choose a type of music and create the tune for this song.

2. How does the style of music enhance the meaning of the song?

_____

_____

_____

_____

_____

_____

_____

_____

_____

_____

_____

_____

3. Then, sing the song for your class.

A Definition of a Warrior

Objective

√ Students will read a passage fluently and accurately using the call-and-response method.

Preparation

- Copy *The Warrior* (page 152) for the teacher.
- Copy *The Warrior—Call and Response* (page 153) for each student.
- For optional use, copy *I Am No Chief* (page 154) for each student.

Fluency Suggestions and Activities

You may want to complete the history and vocabulary activities on the following page before starting this fluency activity. An understanding of the historical context and vocabulary will help students analyze and read the piece fluently.

Note: You might want to have students perform this reading during National American Indian Heritage Month in November.

1. Place a large sheet of paper at the front of the room and ask students to give you a definition of a warrior. Then have students look in dictionaries to see how the word is defined.

2. Tell students that you have a definition of this term from a famous American Indian named Sitting Bull. Read *The Warrior* (page 152) aloud, modeling a fluent reading. Have students compare their definitions to what Sitting Bull said.

3. Give each student a copy of *The Warrior—Call and Response* (page 153) and read it aloud together several times. Model reading lines with changes in pitch, tone, and timing to achieve different effects. Although this is a quote, you are treating it like a poem.

4. Tell students that they will be performing this reading for the janitors and secretaries in your school. This is a great way for the students to get to know those who really keep the school running. Make arrangements ahead of time to accommodate their schedules.

5. Place students into groups of nine students each to read the statement together. Allow time for the students to practice reading the statement several times.

6. When each group feels comfortable, have each of them perform a reading of this statement for one of the janitors and secretaries in your school.

A Definition of a Warrior *(cont.)*

History Connection

Introduce Sitting Bull's statement using the information provided below.

When Sitting Bull was a child, he did everything very carefully. People named him Hunk-es-ni, which means Slow. In time, though, Slow proved that he was not slow minded. He learned the meaning of a warrior from his elders. When he was just 10 years old, he killed his first buffalo. Then, in a battle, he used a coup stick carved from bone given to him by his father. He crept up close to his enemy and then touched him with this coup stick. Anyone who was brave enough to do this was considered a hero of the battle. When his father heard about this, he gave Slow his name, Ta-tan-ka Yo-tan-ka, which means Sitting Bull. Then his father took a new name, Jumping Bull.

Vocabulary Connection

Discuss unfamiliar vocabulary encountered in the text. Some possible words are listed below. After identifying the difficult words, discuss them within the context of the text.

- **sacrifices**—when someone gives up his or her life for something they believe in
- **elderly**—old
- **humanity**—the human race

Extension Ideas

- Have students conduct a survey around the school concerning the definition of a warrior. As they survey, they can have those they are surveying write out their definitions. Then students can take this information and make comparisons to what Sitting Bull said and to their own definitions.

- Distribute copies of *I Am No Chief* (page 154) to students. Have them practice Sitting Bull's statement to the *New York Herald*, as if they are Sitting Bull. Then, allow students to tape record their statement and play it for the class. Take a class vote to decide on who has the most effective voice for Sitting Bull.

The Warrior

By Sitting Bull

For us, warriors are not what you think of as warriors. The warrior is not someone who fights, because no one has the right to take another's life. The warrior, for us, is one who sacrifices himself for the good of others. His task is to take care of the elderly, the defenseless, those who cannot provide for themselves, and above all, the children, the future of humanity.

—Sitting Bull

Name _____

The Warrior—Call and Response

All: **What is a warrior?**

R1: For us, warriors are not what you think of as warriors.

All: **What is a warrior?**

R2: The warrior is not someone who fights

All: **What is a warrior?**

R3: because no one has the right to take another's life.

All: **What is a warrior?**

R4: The warrior, for us, is one who sacrifices himself for the good of others.

All: **What is a warrior?**

R5: His task is to take care of the elderly.

All: **What is a warrior?**

R6: His task is to take care of the defenseless.

All: **What is a warrior?**

R7: His task is to take care of those who cannot provide for themselves.

All: **What is a warrior?**

R8: And above all, his task is to take care of the children.

All: **What is a warrior?**

R9: Take care of the children because they are the future of humanity.

All: **What is a warrior?**

Name _____

I Am No Chief

By Sitting Bull

I am no chief.

I am a man. I see. I know.

I began to see when I was not yet born; when I was not in my mother's
arms, but inside of my mother's belly.

It was there that I began to study about my people.

God gave me the power to see out of the womb.

The Great Spirit must have told me at that time that I would be the man
to be the judge of all the other Indians—a big man, to decide for
them in all their ways.

I speak. It is enough.

I never taught my people to trust Americans.

I have told them the truth - that the Americans are great liars.

I have never dealt with the Americans. Why should I?

The land belonged to my people.

Sitting Bull, New York Herald,
November 16, 1877

Directions: Practice reading the words from Sitting Bull above. Be sure to use
your voice to convey his message. After practicing it several times, tape record
yourself reading it as if you are Sitting Bull. You will play it for your class, and the
class will vote on the most effective voice for Sitting Bull.

Addressing Freedom

Objective

√ Students will participate in cooperative learning and improve expressive reading skills by engaging in reader's theater.

Preparation

- Copy *The Gettysburg Address* (page 157) for each student.
- Copy *The Gettysburg Address—Reader's Theater* (page 158) for each student.
- For optional use, copy *The Gettysburg Address in Song* (page 159) for each student.
- Provide highlighters.

Fluency Suggestions and Activities

You may want to complete the history and vocabulary activities on the following page before starting this fluency activity. An understanding of the historical context and vocabulary will help students analyze and read the piece fluently.

Note: You might want to plan to complete this fluency activity around November 19, which is the date Lincoln presented this speech in Gettysburg, Pennsylvania.

1. Distribute a copy of *The Gettysburg Address* (page 157) and model a fluent reading of it for the students. Tell students that they will be reading this for a group of veterans. Contact the local veterans agency in your town and have students send personal invitations to those veterans.

2. Give each student a copy of *The Gettysburg Address—Reader's Theater* (page 158). Place students into groups of five. Assign parts to students by having them volunteer or audition. Have students highlight their parts.

3. Read the script together several times. Model reading lines with changes in pitch, tone, and timing to achieve different effects. Ask students to look for clues in the text that tell them how to read it.

4. Students then begin to read their assigned parts aloud. Provide time for practice individually, with partners, and in small groups.

5. Students should then practice their parts with their whole groups. Once the students are comfortable, have them perform their readings for the invited veterans.

Addressing Freedom (cont.)

History Connection

Discuss the history of the Gettysburg Address using the information below.

From July 1–3, 1863, a large battle was fought between the Union and Confederate forces in Gettysburg, Pennsylvania. The fighting ended with more than 50,000 dead. The dead were soon buried there and in November, Abraham Lincoln was invited to dedicate the battlefield as a national cemetery. Lincoln stood and gave his short speech. It had only 237 words and just 10 sentences. Incidentally, his short speech followed a two-hour speech given by another man. It was Lincoln's desire to give meaning to the death of these men and to explain that the Constitution meant equality for all men, black or white.

Vocabulary Connection

Discuss unfamiliar vocabulary encountered in the text. Some possible words are listed below. After identifying the difficult words, discuss them within the context of the text.

- **fourscore**—80 years; or four times a score, which is 20 years
- **proposition**—idea
- **conceived**—begun
- **endure**—last through the years
- **dedicate**—to set apart or assign a special use for something
- **propriety**—true nature
- **consecrate**—to honor
- **hallow**—to make holy or sacred
- **detract**—take away from
- **devotion**—religious beliefs
- **perish**—to die

Extension Ideas

- Have students work in groups of two to create a multimedia slide show that explains the Gettysburg Address. Allow students to present their slide shows for different classes that are studying the Civil War or Abraham Lincoln.

- Distribute copies of *The Gettysburg Address in Song* (page 159). On this page, students will be using sections from the Gettysburg Address and creating a verse for a song. There will be four verses in all. Allow students to read or sing their songs for the class.

The Gettysburg Address

Abraham Lincoln—November 19, 1863

Fourscore and seven years ago our fathers brought forth on this continent a new nation, conceived in liberty and dedicated to the proposition that all men are created equal.

Now we are engaged in a great civil war, testing whether that nation or any nation so conceived and so dedicated can long endure. We are met on a great battlefield of that war. We have come to dedicate a portion of it as a final resting place for those who died here that the nation might live. This we may, in all propriety do. But in a larger sense, we cannot dedicate, we cannot consecrate, we cannot hallow this ground. The brave men, living and dead who struggled here have hallowed it far above our poor power to add or detract. The world will little note nor long remember what we say here, but it can never forget what they did here.

It is rather for us the living, we here be dedicated to the great task remaining before us—that from these honored dead we take increased devotion to that cause for which they here gave the last full measure of devotion—that we here highly resolve that these dead shall not have died in vain, that this nation shall have a new birth of freedom, and that government of the people, by the people, for the people shall not perish from the earth.

Name _____

The Gettysburg Address— Reader's Theater

R1: Fourscore and seven years ago

R2: our fathers brought forth on this continent a new nation,

R3: conceived in liberty and dedicated to the proposition

All: **that all men are created equal.**

R4: Now we are engaged in a great civil war,

R5: testing whether that nation or any nation so conceived and so dedicated can long endure.

R1: We are met on a great battlefield of that war.

R2: We have come to dedicate a portion of it as a final resting place

R3: for those who died here that the nation might live.

R4: This we may, in all propriety do.

All: **But in a larger sense, we cannot dedicate, we cannot consecrate, we cannot hallow this ground.**

R5: The brave men, living and dead who struggled here

R1: have hallowed it far above our poor power to add or detract.

R2: The world will little note nor long remember what we say here,

All: **but it can never forget what they did here.**

R3: It is rather for us the living,

R4: we here be dedicated to the great task remaining before us—

R5: that from these honored dead we take increased devotion

R1: to that cause for which they here gave the last full measure of devotion—

R2: that we here highly resolve that these dead shall not have died in vain,

R3: that this nation shall have a new birth of freedom,

All: **and that government of the people, by the people, for the people shall not perish from the earth.**

Name _____

The Gettysburg Address in Song

Directions: Look at your copy of the Gettysburg Address. How can the message of the Gettysburg Address be written as a song? There will be four verses in all. Take each section below and write a verse for it. Then put them all together to form your song on the Gettysburg Address. Read it or add a tune and sing it for your classmates.

1. Fourscore and seven years ago our fathers brought forth on this continent a new nation, conceived in liberty and dedicated to the proposition that all men are created equal.

   _____

   _____

   _____

2. Now we are engaged in a great civil war, testing whether that nation or any nation so conceived and so dedicated can long endure. We are met on a great battlefield of that war. We have come to dedicate a portion of it as a final resting place for those who died here that the nation might live. This we may, in all propriety do.

   _____

   _____

   _____

   _____

3. But in a larger sense, we cannot dedicate, we cannot consecrate, we cannot hallow this ground. The brave men, living and dead who struggled here have hallowed it far above our poor power to add or detract. The world will little note nor long remember what we say here, but it can never forget what they did here.

   _____

   _____

   _____

   _____

4. It is rather for us the living, we here be dedicated to the great task remaining before us—that from these honored dead we take increased devotion to that cause for which they here gave the last full measure of devotion—that we here highly resolve that these dead shall not have died in vain, that this nation shall have a new birth of freedom, and that government of the people, by the people, for the people shall not perish from the earth.

   _____

   _____

   _____

   _____

The Captain!

Objective

- Students will participate in cooperative learning and improve expressive reading skills by engaging in reader's theater.

Preparation

- Copy the poem, "O Captain! My Captain!" (page 162), for the teacher.
- Copy *"O Captain! My Captain!"—Reader's Theater* (pages 163–168) for each student.
- Provide highlighters.

Fluency Suggestions and Activities

You may want to complete the history and vocabulary activities on the following page before starting this fluency activity. An understanding of the historical context and vocabulary will help students analyze and read the piece fluently.

Note: You might want to plan to complete this fluency activity on President's Day, Abraham Lincoln's birthday, or on April 14, the anniversary of Lincoln's assassination.

1. Model a fluent reading of the poem, "O Captain! My Captain!" (page 162), for the students.

2. Give each student a copy of *"O Captain! My Captain!"—Reader's Theater* (pages 163–168). Tell students that they will be performing this poem for classes within their school. Place students in groups of four. Assign parts to students by having them volunteer or audition. Have students highlight their parts.

3. Read the script together several times. Model reading lines with changes in pitch, tone, and timing to achieve different effects. Ask students to look for clues in the text that tell them how to read it (e.g., commas or exclamation points).

4. Students then begin to read their assigned parts aloud. Provide time for practice individually, with partners, and in small groups.

5. Students should then practice their parts with groups of four. Once the students are comfortable, have them perform their readings for other classes within the school.

The Captain! (cont.)

History Connection

Discuss the history of "O Captain! My Captain!" using the information below.

Walt Whitman wrote this poem after Abraham Lincoln was assassinated in 1865. It was said that the night before the assassination, Whitman dreamed of a ship coming into a harbor with full sails. This poem was published in the New York City *Saturday Press* and became Whitman's most famous poem during his lifetime. When Whitman had a speaking engagement, he was always asked to recite it. This happened so many times that he once said that he almost wished he had never written it.

Vocabulary Connection

Discuss unfamiliar vocabulary encountered in the text. Some possible words are listed below. After identifying the difficult words, discuss them within the context of the text.

- **rack**—wind-driven storm
- **sought**—looked for
- **exulting**—celebrating
- **keel**—a ship with a flat bottom much like a barge
- **vessel**—a ship or boat
- **trills**—a musical tone with vibrations
- **victor**—victorious
- **tread**—to walk

Extension Idea

- Discuss the meanings of words with unusual spellings, such as weather'd, ribbon'd, and anchor'd. Display these words on the board and ask the students to determine the pronunciation of each. Explain that while these words may seem unfamiliar at first glance, most are familiar words, when spelled in a conventional manner. They are often spelled this way in poems and song lyrics for the purposes of flow and rhythm.

O Captain! My Captain!

By Walt Whitman

O Captain! my Captain! Our fearful trip is done;
The ship has weather'd every rack, the prize we sought is won;
The port is near, the bells I hear, the people all exulting,
While follow eyes the steady keel, the vessel grim and daring.
But O heart! heart! heart!
O the bleeding drops of red!
Where on the deck my captain lies,
Fallen cold and dead.

O Captain! my Captain! Rise up and hear the bells;
Rise up—for you the flag is flung—for you the bugle trills;
For you bouquets and ribbon'd wreaths—for you the shores a-crowding;
For you they call, the swaying mass, their eager faces turning.
Here Captain! dear father!
The arm beneath your head,
It is some dream that on the deck
You've fallen cold and dead.

My Captain does not answer, his lips are pale and still:
My father does not feel my arm, he has no pulse nor will.
The ship is anchor'd safe and sound, its voyage closed and done:
From fearful trip the victor ship comes in with object won!
Exult O shores, and ring O bells!
But I with silent tread,
Walk the deck my captain lies
Fallen cold and dead.

Name _____

"O Captain! My Captain!"— Reader's Theater

All: **O Captain! my Captain!**

R1:   Abraham Lincoln was once the captain of our great nation.

All: **Our fearful trip is done;**

R2:   The Union had just experienced the Civil War.

R3:   Brothers fought against brothers

R4:   Friends battled against friends.

R1:   The North won and the war was finally over.

All: **The ship has weathered every rack, the prize we sought is won;**

R2:   The ship was the Union

R3:   and it made it through the painful years of war.

R4:   The prize was winning the war and keeping the Union together.

All: **The port is near,**

R1:   The port signals peace between the North and South.

R2:   Even with the war over, there is much work to do to end the division.

R3:   That's why the port is near, and they have not arrived at the port yet.

"O Captain! My Captain!"— Reader's Theater *(cont.)*

All: **the bells I hear,**

R4:   The bells are ones of victory.

All: **the people all exulting,**

R1:   All the people are happy about hearing the bells of victory.

All: **While follow eyes the steady keel, the vessel grim and daring.**

R2:   On the shore the people are looking at this ship,

R3:   which is the Union,

R4:   which shows the wear from four long years of battle.

R1:   Lincoln undertook the brave task of fighting to keep the Union together.

All: **But O heart! heart! heart!**

R2:   Pay attention! Something terrible has happened!

All: **O the bleeding drops of red,**

R3:   The blood of all the dead,

R4:   including soldiers who fought for the cause

R1:   and Lincoln who fought to keep the Union together

R2:   is on the deck of the ship.

All: **Where on the deck my Captain lies,**

"O Captain! My Captain!"— Reader's Theater *(cont.)*

All: **Fallen cold and dead.**

R3:   Lincoln, the captain, is dead.

All: **O Captain! my Captain! Rise up and hear the bells;**

R4:   Lincoln! Get up! Get up!

R1:   I can't believe you are not alive!

R2:   Which bells do you hear?

R3:   Are they the bells of victory?

R4:   Or do you hear the bells of death?

All: **Rise up—for you the flag is flung—for you the bugle trills;**

R1:   The flag is flying.

R2:   Is it flying for your victory or for your death?

R3:   The horn is playing for you.

R4:   Is it playing for your victory or for your death?

All: **For you bouquets and ribboned wreaths—**

R1:   Flowers and wreaths are everywhere.

R2:   Is this a victory parade

R3:   or a funeral procession?

"O Captain! My Captain!"— Reader's Theater (cont.)

All: **for you the shores a-crowding;**

R4: Everyone is crowding around the shore in honor of you.

All: **For you they call, the swaying mass, their eager faces turning.**

R1: The masses of people are calling for you.

R2: The eager faces hope to see their captain, their leader.

All: **Here Captain! dear father!**

R3: The captain, Lincoln, was a father to the Union.

R4: It was this father's determination that kept the Union together.

All: **The arm beneath your head!**

R1: His wife held him in her arms after he was shot.

All: **It is some dream that on the deck**

R2: Your dream of keeping the nation together

R3: Has brought you nothing but death.

All: **You've fallen cold and dead.**

R4: Their leader, the president, has lost his life for the peace of this country.

"O Captain! My Captain!"— Reader's Theater *(cont.)*

All: **My Captain does not answer, his lips are pale and still:**

R1: Lincoln cannot provide the answers anymore

R2: because he is dead.

R3: It's someone else's turn to lead our country

R4: and give us the answers we need.

All: **My father does not feel my arm, he has no pulse nor will.**

R1: Lincoln did all he could to lead us.

R2: He gave everything

R3: including his life

R4: for his country.

R1: Now that Lincoln is dead,

R2: leadership and meaning for our country must be found somewhere else.

All: **The ship is anchored safe and sound,**

R3: Thanks to Lincoln

R4: everything America once stood for is now secure again.

"O Captain! My Captain!"— Reader's Theater *(cont.)*

All: **its voyage closed and done:**

R1: The war is over

R2: and the North and South reunite in one strong Union.

All: **From fearful trip the victor ship comes in with object won!**

R3: The war brought fear with brothers fighting brothers.

R4: But the war is now over and the Union can focus on being a great nation again.

All: **Exult O shores, and ring O bells!**

R1: Sing Lincoln's praises!

R2: He did a great thing in saving our nation.

R3: Are the bells of celebration,

R4: or bells of death?

All: **But I with silent tread,**

R1: While the country is celebrating the end of the war,

R2: I must mourn the loss of Lincoln.

All: **Walk the deck my captain lies**

R3: Now I have to live in this Union

R4: where the life of Lincoln, the leader, was taken.

All: **Fallen cold and dead.**

Lee and the Civil War

Objective

√ Students will deliver a group oral presentation and read passages fluently with changes in tone, voice, timing, and expression using call-and-response method.

Preparation

- Make an overhead transparency of *A Letter Explaining Lee's Decision* (page 171).
- Copy *A Letter Explaining Lee's Decision—Call and Response* (page 172) for each student.

Fluency Suggestions and Activities

You may want to complete the history and vocabulary activities on the following page before starting this fluency activity. An understanding of the historical context and vocabulary will help students analyze and read the piece fluently.

Note: You might want to complete this reading activity around April 12, to remember the beginning of the Civil War.

1. Place a transparency copy of *A Letter Explaining Lee's Decision* (page 171) on the overhead. Read it aloud, modeling fluent reading. Explain that this is a letter that General Robert E. Lee wrote to one of his relatives.

2. Place the students into small groups. Each group will be responsible for presenting an call-and-response reading to the class.

3. Give students a copy of *A Letter Explaining Lee's Decision—Call and Response* (page 172). This sheet has the selection broken into short reading parts. Students will come up with the responses to each selection. In other words, allow the small groups to write their own responses rather than having each group perform the same text. You will probably want to model this with the students to get them started. For example, the first line reads, "In my own person I had to meet the question." Students could have the response be, "meet the question, meet the question." The second line reads, "whether I should take part against my native state." The response could be, "fight against Virginia, fight against Virginia."

4. Challenge students to think about how Robert E. Lee felt when writing this letter. Can they sense anger, sadness, or disgust in his words? Have each group decide how they will read it based on emotion.

5. On the day of the presentations, have each group perform its reading. If desired, students can use hand motions and facial expressions as they read. Remind them that they want to get the audience involved emotionally in the presentation of the letter. Then, after all the groups have presented, take a vote on which group gave the most dramatic performance. You might want to tell students that they cannot vote for their own groups.

Lee and the Civil War (cont.)

History Connection

Introduce Robert E. Lee using the information provided below.

Robert E. Lee attended West Point Military Academy and sought a career in the military. Lee served his country as an engineer in the Mexican War, the superintendent of West Point, and even settled disputes concerning the Indians in Texas. When the Civil War began, Lee returned to Virginia. At the recommendation of Winfield Scott, Abraham Lincoln asked Lee to command the Union army. Lee struggled with this decision, but after hearing that Virginia voted to secede, he declined the offer and sent in his resignation to the Union army. Leaving the military was a very hard decision for Lee to make. This job was all he knew how to do, and he loved serving his country in that way. This letter was written to a relative and tells why Lee chose to side with the Confederacy.

Vocabulary Connection

Discuss unfamiliar vocabulary encountered in the text. Some possible words are listed below. After identifying the difficult words, discuss them within the context of the text.

- **forborne**—held back
- **redress of grievances**—make up for complaints
- **native**—the place where he was born, his home
- **devotion**—loyalty
- **resigned**—left a job
- **commission**—specific job title and responsibilities
- **sincere**—truthful or heartfelt
- **endeavored**—tried

Extension Idea

- Have students respond to Lee's letter as if they are his relative. What would they say to him? Would they agree or disagree with his decision? Allow students to first practice reading their letters, and then, let them perform their readings for their classmates.

A Letter Explaining Lee's Decision

By Robert E. Lee

Arlington, Virginia, April 20, 1861

My Dear Sister,

I am grieved at my inability to see you . . . I have been waiting "for a more convenient season," which has brought to many before me deep and lasting regret. Now we are in a state of war, which will yield to nothing. The whole South is in a state of revolution, into which Virginia, after a long struggle, has been drawn; and though I recognize no necessity for this state of things, and would have forborne and pleaded to the end for redress of grievances, real or supposed, yet, in my own person, I had to meet the question, whether I should take part against my native State.

With all my devotion to the Union, and the feeling of loyalty and duty of an American citizen, I have not been able to make up my mind to raise my hand against my relatives, my children, my home. I have, therefore, resigned my commission in the army; and save in defence of my native State, with the sincere hope that my poor services may never be needed, I hope I may never be called on to draw my sword.

I know you will blame me; but you must think as kindly of me as you can, and believe that I have endeavored to do what I thought right. To show you the feeling and struggle it has cost me, I send a copy of my letter to Gen. Scott, which accompanied my letter of resignation. I have no time for more . . . May God guard and protect you and yours, and shower upon you everlasting blessings, is the prayer of your devoted brother,

R. E. Lee

Name _____

A Letter Explaining Lee's Decision—Call and Response

Directions: Work with your group to come up with responses for each of these lines from Robert E. Lee's letter. You can make them long or short. It doesn't matter as long as you like how they sound when you read them aloud.

In my own person, I had to meet the question

_____

whether I should take part against my native state.

_____

With all my devotion to the Union,

_____

and the feeling of loyalty and duty as an American citizen,

_____

I have not been able to make up my mind

_____

to raise my hand against my relatives, my children, or my home.

_____

I have, therefore, resigned my commission in the Army,

_____

and, save in defense of my native state,

_____

with the sincere hope that my poor services may never be needed,

_____

I hope I may never be called upon to draw my sword.

_____

Saying Farewell

Objective

- Students will participate in cooperative learning and improve expressive reading skills by engaging in reader's theater.

Preparation

- Copy *Lee's Farewell to the Army of Northern Virginia* (page 175) for the teacher.
- Copy *Lee's Farewell to the Army of Northern Virginia—Reader's Theater* (pages 176–178) for each student.
- For optional use, copy *To the People of Maryland* (page 179) for each student.
- Provide highlighters.

Fluency Suggestions and Activities

You may want to complete the history and vocabulary activities on the following page before starting this fluency activity. An understanding of the historical context and vocabulary will help students analyze and read the piece fluently.

Note: Have students perform this reading around the time of Palm Sunday, the day that Lee actually surrendered.

1. Model a fluent reading of *Lee's Farewell to the Army of Northern Virginia* (page 175) for the students. Tell the students that they will be performing this speech for the workers in the school cafeteria.

2. Give each student a copy of *Lee's Farewell to the Army of Northern Virginia—Reader's Theater* (pages 176–178). There are six parts in this reader's theater. Assign parts to students by having them volunteer or audition. Have students highlight their parts. To allow more students to participate, divide the parts into more groups to allow the entire class to participate in the reading or allow more than one group to perform the reading.

3. Read the script together several times. Model reading lines with changes in pitch, tone, and timing to achieve different effects. Ask students to look for clues in the text that tell them how to read it (e.g., commas or periods).

4. Students then begin to read their assigned parts aloud in small groups. Provide time for practice.

5. Once the students are comfortable, have them perform their readings for the cafeteria workers in your school.

Saying Farewell *(cont.)*

History Connection

Introduce Lee's Farewell using the information provided below.

On April 10, 1865, Robert E. Lee gave his final order to the Army of Northern Virginia. Just the day before, he had surrendered this army to General Grant. Both General Lee and General Grant rode to Appomattox Court House to talk about the surrender. Lee arrived dressed in his best uniform with a sash and a sword at his side. Grant arrived directly from the field with mud-spattered pants and boots. Grant wrote up generous terms of surrender. All he really asked was that the Confederate soldiers surrender their guns and go to their homes. The Southern officers could keep both their guns and their horses. Grant also promised that the leaders would not be charged with treason. Lee felt the heavy weight of his army's suffering. Although he believed in protecting his native land of Virginia, he knew his men could not go on any longer. In this speech, Lee tells the reasons why he had to surrender. He shows his love and admiration for these devoted men who fought until the end and praises their courage and diligence. At last, he encourages them to go back home and prays for their protection.

Vocabulary Connection

Discuss unfamiliar vocabulary encountered in the text. Some possible words are listed below. After identifying the difficult words, discuss them within the context of the text.

- **arduous**—difficult or hard
- **unsurpassed**—not passed by others
- **fortitude**—strength or courage
- **compelled**—forced
- **yield**—to give in
- **steadfast**—committed and unswerving
- **consented**—agreed to
- **valor**—bravery and courage
- **compensate**—to make up for
- **continuance**—continuing
- **sacrifice**—losing for no reason
- **constancy**—loyalty

Extension Idea

- Distribute copies of *To the People of Maryland* (page 179) to the students. Explain that this was also written by Robert E. Lee. Have students work with partners to write their own reader's theaters using this piece.

Lee's Farewell to the Army of Northern Virginia

By Robert E. Lee

After four years of arduous service, marked by unsurpassed courage and fortitude, the Army of Northern Virginia has been compelled to yield to overwhelming numbers and resources.

I need not tell the survivors of so many hard-fought battles who have remained steadfast to the last that I have consented to this result from no distrust of them; but feeling that valor and devotion could accomplish nothing that could compensate for the loss that would have attended the continuance of the contest, I determined to avoid the useless sacrifice of those whose past services have endeared them to their countrymen. By the terms of the agreement, officers and men can return to their homes and remain until exchanged.

You may take with you the satisfaction that proceeds from the consciousness of duty faithfully performed, and I earnestly pray that a merciful God will extend to you his blessing and protection.

With an unceasing admiration of your constancy and devotion to your country, and a grateful remembrance of your kind and generous consideration of myself, I bid you all an affectionate farewell.

Name _____

Lee's Farewell to the Army of Northern Virginia—Reader's Theater

All: **After four years of arduous service,**

R1: We've served four difficult years in this war

All: **marked by unsurpassed courage and fortitude,**

R2: I've never met any men more courageous

R3: and with more guts and strength than all of you.

All: **the Army of Northern Virginia**

R4: the men I've led in this Civil War

All: **has been compelled to yield to overwhelming numbers and resources.**

R5: We've been forced to give in to the Union

R6: because they have more men

R1: and more food

R2: and more ammunition.

All: **I need not tell the survivors of so many hard-fought battles who have remained steadfast to the last that I have consented to this result from no distrust of them;**

R3: I don't need to tell you,

R4: the ones who have survived fighting the battles,

Lee's Farewell to the Army of Northern Virginia—Reader's Theater *(cont.)*

R5: the ones who have been committed to fighting the battles,

R6: that my decision has nothing to do with a fear that you won't continue to fight.

All: **but feeling that valor and devotion could accomplish nothing that could compensate for the loss that would have attended the continuance of the contest,**

R1: Your courage and spirit cannot make up for the deaths that would continue

R2: if the war were to drag on.

All: **I determined to avoid the useless sacrifice of those whose past services have endeared them to their countrymen.**

R3: It would be wrong for me to ask you to die

R4: when I know that we cannot win this war.

All: **By the terms of the agreement, officers and men can return to their homes and remain until exchanged.**

R5: The terms of agreement say

R6: all the officers

R1: and all the men

R2: can go home to their families now.

Lee's Farewell to the Army of Northern Virginia—Reader's Theater *(cont.)*

All: **You may take with you the satisfaction that proceeds from the consciousness of duty faithfully performed,**

R3: You can hold your head high and be proud

R4: that you've been faithful soliders, performing your duty to the end.

All: **and I earnestly pray that a merciful God will extend to you his blessing and protection.**

R5: I pray that God will

R6: protect and bless you.

All: **With an unceasing admiration of your constancy and devotion to your country,**

R1: I admire your steadiness,

R2: your faithfulness,

R3: and your loyalty

R4: and I myself will remain devoted to our great country.

All: **and a grateful remembrance of your kind and generous consideration of myself,**

R5: I will always remember how kind you were to me, your leader.

All: **I bid you all an affectionate farewell.**

R6: I will now say goodbye.

Name _____

To the People of Maryland

By Robert E. Lee

September 8, 1862

To the People of Maryland,

It is right that you should know the purpose that brought the army under my command within the limits of your State, so far as that purpose concerns yourselves.

The people of the Confederate States have long watched with the deepest sympathy the wrongs and outrages that have been inflicted upon the citizens of a commonwealth allied to the States of the South by the strongest social, political, and commercial ties.

. . . Believing that the people of Maryland possessed a spirit too lofty to submit to such a government, the people of the South have long wished to aid you in throwing off this foreign yoke, to enable you again to enjoy the inalienable rights of freemen, and restore independence and sovereignty to your State.

In obedience to this wish, our army has come among you, and is prepared to assist you with the power of its arms in regaining the rights of which you have been despoiled.

. . . We know no enemies among you, and will protect all, of every opinion. It is for you to decide your destiny freely and without constraint. This army will respect your choice, whatever it may be; and while the Southern people will rejoice to welcome you to your natural position among them, they will only welcome you when you come of your own free will.

R. E. LEE, General, Commanding

Directions: Lee wrote this letter to the people of Maryland when the Southern army moved north into that state 1862. The text above is an excerpt of the whole letter. Use this text to create an interesting reader's theater. On other paper, create a reader's theater that shares this text and explains it to the audience.

The Warrior Grant

Objective

√ Students will read "On a Great Warrior" as a divided reading.

Preparation

- Make an overhead transparency of the poem, "On a Great Warrior" (page 182).
- Copy *"On a Great Warrior"—Divided Reading* (page 183) for each student.

Fluency Suggestions and Activities

You may want to complete the history and vocabulary activities on the following page before starting this fluency activity. An understanding of the historical context and vocabulary will help students analyze and read the piece fluently.

Note: You might want to complete this activity on Ulysses S. Grant's birthday, April 27.

1. Place the transparency of the poem "On a Great Warrior" (page 182), on the overhead and read it aloud, modeling fluent reading for the students.

2. Give each student a copy of *"On a Great Warrior"—Divided Reading* (page 183) and read it aloud together several times. Model reading lines with changes in pitch, tone, and timing to achieve different effects.

3. Tell students that they will perform a reading of this poem during lunch in the lunchroom of the school.

4. Divide students into five groups. Each group will be responsible for reading one stanza of the poem. Allow time for the students to practice the poem several times.

5. When the class feels comfortable, have them perform a reading of this poem to other students who are studying the Civil War. Allow students to share the background information about Grant and to answer questions their audience might have about this warrior.

The Warrior Grant (cont.)

History Connection

Introduce Ulysses S. Grant using the information provided below.

Ulysses S. Grant was a graduate of West Point. He served in the Mexican War and then went into the business world. No one really expected much of Grant when the Civil War began. On the battlefield, he did not care much for his appearance, but Grant was a determined leader. He knew how to stand his ground and defeat his enemy in battle. It was at the Battle of Shiloh in Tennessee that he earned national fame. He then held Vicksburg, Mississippi, under siege for almost a year before accepting their surrender. Grant took Chattanooga, Tennessee, from the South and one by one, the cities surrendered to him. In April 1864, Lincoln named him the commander of the entire Northern army. One year later, the war was over. He was elected president after the war, but his two terms were filled with scandals. Unfortunately, it seems that fighting battles was the only thing that Grant did well, but he did that very well.

Vocabulary Connection

Discuss unfamiliar vocabulary encountered in the text. Some possible words are listed below. After identifying the difficult words, discuss them within the context of the text.

- **wrung**—squeezed or filled
- **serene**—calmly
- **smote**—defeated
- **bade**—commanded
- **yoke**—to control, burden
- **shackles**—chains or restraints
- **mien**—the look or appearance
- **garish**—showy
- **clime**—region

Extension Idea

- Have students create a collage that goes along with this poem about Grant. Provide magazines, newspapers, and old books with pictures that can be cut out. Let students decorate a bulletin board with this collage as a dedication to Grant.

On a Great Warrior

By Henry Abbey

When all the sky was wild and dark,
When every heart was wrung with
   fear,
He rose serene, and took his place,
The great occasion's mighty peer.
He smote armed opposition down,
He bade the storm and darkness
   cease,
And o'er the long-distracted land
Shone out the smiling sun of peace.

The famous captains of the past
March in review before the mind;
Some fought for glory, some for gold,
But most to yoke and rule mankind.
Not so the captain, great of soul,
At peace within the granite grave;
He fought to keep the Union whole,
And break the shackles of the slaves.

A silent man, in friendship true,
He made point-blank his certain aim,
And, born a stranger to defeat,
To steadfast purpose linked his name.
He followed duty with the mien
Of but a soldier in the ranks,
This God-sent man that saved the
   State,
And conquered its victorious thanks.

How well he wore white honor's
   flower,
The gratitude and praise of men,
As General, as President,
And then as simple citizen!
He was a hero to the end!
The dark rebellion raised by death
Against the powers of life and light,
He battled hard, with failing breath.

O hero of Fort Donelson,
And wooded Shiloh's frightful strife!
Sleep on! for honor loves the tomb
More than the garish ways of life.
Sleep on! sleep on! Thy wondrous days
Fill freedom's most illustrious page.
Long-mem'ried Fame shall sound thy
   praise
In every clime, in every age.

Name _____

"On a Great Warrior"— Divided Reading

G1: When all the sky was wild and dark,
When every heart was wrung with
  fear,
He rose serene, and took his place,
The great occasion's mighty peer.
He smote armed opposition down,
He bade the storm and darkness
  cease,
And o'er the long-distracted land
Shone out the smiling sun of peace.

G2: The famous captains of the past
March in review before the mind;
Some fought for glory, some for
  gold,
But most to yoke and rule mankind.
Not so the captain, great of soul,
At peace within the granite grave;
He fought to keep the Union whole,
And break the shackles of the
  slaves.

G3: A silent man, in friendship true,
He made point-blank his certain
  aim,
And, born a stranger to defeat,
To steadfast purpose linked his
  name.
He followed duty with the mien
Of but a soldier in the ranks,
This God-sent man that saved the
  State,
And conquered its victorious thanks.

G4: How well he wore white honor's
  flower,
The gratitude and praise of men,
As General, as President,
And then as simple citizen!
He was a hero to the end!
The dark rebellion raised by death
Against the powers of life and light,
He battled hard, with failing breath.

G5: O hero of Fort Donelson,
And wooded Shiloh's frightful strife!
Sleep on! for honor loves the tomb
More than the garish ways of life.
Sleep on! sleep on! Thy wondrous
  days
Fill freedom's most illustrious page.
Long-mem'ried Fame shall sound
  thy praise
In every clime, in every age.

In Grant's Own Words

Objective

√ Students will practice reading aloud portions of text in preparation for public performances.

Preparation

- Copy *Grant's Memoirs* (pages 186–187) for the teacher.
- Copy *Grant's Memoirs—Divided Reading* (pages 188–192) for each student.

Fluency Suggestions and Activities

You may want to complete the history and vocabulary activities on the following page before starting this fluency activity. An understanding of the historical context and vocabulary will help students analyze and read the piece fluently.

1. Ask students if they know the definition of a *memoir*. If students don't know, have them look it up in dictionaries and share the definition with the class. If possible, have a copy of Grant's memoirs on hand to show students the whole book.

2. Tell students that you are going to read a few sections from Grant's book. Read *Grant's Memoirs* (pages 186–187) to the class, modeling fluency.

3. Distribute copies of *Grant's Memoirs—Divided Reading* (pages 188–192) to students. Tell students that they will be performing these readings on the school's loudspeaker. There are enough sections to allow for 10 days of performances.

4. Divide students into 10 groups. Each group will be responsible for reading a section on the loudspeaker. They can divide their portion into sections so that every student in their group has an opportunity to speak.

5. Remind the students to think about how to use their voices to make the written sections interesting. Allow the students several days in class to practice the reading of their sections of the memoirs. To practice their presentations, have students present their sections of the memoirs to the rest of the class. Encourage classmates to offer suggestions for improved fluency.

6. Shortly before the performances, have each group add a few sentences before and after the text to introduce and conclude the reading. For example, the students reading the first section might say, "The following is a section from Ulysses S. Grant's memoirs. He wrote this to explain how nervous he was just before his first fight in the Civil War. Harris is a confederate leader who Grant faces in this first battle." To conclude, students might say, "This concludes our reading of Grant's memoirs today."

In Grant's Own Words (cont.)

History Connection

Introduce Grant's memoirs using the information provided below.

War heroes usually made great candidates for public office, and Grant was no exception. He was elected to two terms as president of the United States. But his years in office were marked with scandal. Grant had good intentions, but he was naïve and trusted people too much. Wealthy men took advantage of him, and he was relieved when his two terms ended. He and his wife spent his retirement years traveling. When he became sick, his good friend, Mark Twain, convinced him to write his memoirs. He wrote about everything from childhood to his years in the army. Grant finished his book just one week before dying of throat cancer in 1885. His book was an instant best seller and provided the financial security his family needed.

Vocabulary Connection

Discuss unfamiliar vocabulary encountered in the text. Some possible words are listed below. After identifying the difficult words, discuss them within the context of the text.

- **trepidation**—fear
- **mowed**—to cut down
- **sparring**—bickering or squabbling
- **commenced**—began
- **haversacks**—a bag carried over the shoulder
- **procrastination**—to wait, put off, or delay
- **cordially**—friendly
- **picket**—the edge of where the army was encamped

- **tolerate**—to put up with
- **alleviate**—to ease or lessen
- **garrison**—the regiment of troops
- **rendering**—an act of giving
- **effusion**—an outpouring
- **impassible**—cannot be crossed over

Extension Ideas

- If possible, have students look at other entries in Grant's memoirs. Allow them to pick other passages and read them aloud.

- After reading this portion of Grant's memoirs, students should have a good idea of what Grant was like. Have them work in small groups to write a children's book about Ulysses S. Grant. Students can use drawn pictures, clip art, magazine pictures, or pictures on the Internet to illustrate their books. Then, allow them to share their books with students in a younger grade in the school.

Grant's Memoirs

It occurred to me at once that Harris had been as much afraid of me as I had been of him. This was a view of the question I had never taken before; but it was one I never forgot afterwards. From that event to the close of the war, I never experienced trepidation upon confronting an enemy, though I always felt more or less anxiety. I never forgot that he had as much reason to fear my forces as I had his. The lesson was valuable.

—On the anxiety that he felt prior to his first possible
engagement as regiment commander during the Civil War

I saw an open field, in our possession on the second day, over which the Confederates had made repeated charges the day before, so covered with dead that it would have been possible to walk across the clearing, in any direction, stepping on dead bodies, without a foot touching the ground. The enemy fought bravely, but they had started out to defeat and destroy an army and capture a position. They failed in both, with very heavy loss in killed and wounded, and must have gone back discouraged and convinced that the "Yankee" was not an enemy to be despised.

—On the Battle of Shiloh

I always admired the South, as bad as I thought their cause, for the boldness with which they silenced all opposition and all croaking, by press or by individuals, within their control. War at all times, whether a civil war between sections of a common country or between nations, ought to be avoided, if possible with honor. But, once entered into, it is too much for human nature to tolerate an enemy within their ranks to give aid and comfort to the armies of the opposing section or nation. While a battle is raging one can see his enemy mowed down by the thousand, or the ten thousand, with great composure; but after the battle these scenes are distressing, and one is naturally disposed to do as much to alleviate the suffering of an enemy as a friend.

—Following the Battle of Champion's Hill

During the siege there had been a good deal of friendly sparring between the soldiers of the two armies, on picket and where the lines were close together. All rebels were known as "Johnnies," all Union troops as "Yanks." Often "Johnny" would call: "Well, Yank, when are you coming into town?" The reply was sometimes: "We propose to celebrate the 4th of July there." Sometimes it would be: "We always treat our prisoners with kindness and do not want to hurt them;" or, "We are holding you as prisoners of war while you are feeding yourselves." The garrison, from the commanding general down, undoubtedly expected an assault on the fourth. They knew from the temper of their men it would be successful when made; and that would be a greater humiliation than to surrender. Besides it would be attended with severe loss to them.

—On the Siege of Vicksburg

At the appointed hour the garrison of Vicksburg marched out of their works and formed line in front, stacked arms and marched back in good order. Our whole army present witnessed this scene without cheering. Logan's division, which had approached nearest the rebel works, was the first to march in; and the flag of one of the regiments of his division was soon floating over the court-house. Our soldiers were no sooner inside the lines than the two armies began to fraternize. Our men had had full rations from the time the siege commenced, to the close. The enemy had been suffering, particularly towards the last. I myself saw our men taking bread from their haversacks and giving it to the enemy they had so recently been engaged in starving out. It was accepted with avidity and with thanks.

—On the Siege of Vicksburg

Grant's Memoirs *(cont.)*

In my first interview with Mr. Lincoln alone he stated to me that he had never professed to be a military man or to know how campaigns should be conducted, and never wanted to interfere in them: but that procrastination on the part of commanders, and the pressure from the people at the North and Congress, WHICH WAS ALWAYS WITH HIM, forced him into issuing his series of "Military Orders"—one, two, three, etc. He did not know but they were all wrong, and did know that some of them were. All he wanted or had ever wanted was some one who would take the responsibility and act, and call on him for all the assistance needed, pledging himself to use all the power of the government in rendering such assistance. Assuring him that I would do the best I could with the means at hand, and avoid as far as possible annoying him or the War Department, our first interview ended. He always showed a generous and kindly spirit toward the Southern people, and I never heard him abuse an enemy. Some of the cruel things said about President Lincoln, particularly in the North, used to pierce him to the heart; but never in my presence did he evince a revengeful disposition.

—About Abraham Lincoln

The result of the last week must convince you of the hopelessness of further resistance on the part of the Army of Northern Virginia in this struggle. I feel that it is so, and regard it as my duty to shift from myself the responsibility of any further effusion of blood, by asking of you the surrender of that portion of the Confederate States army known as the Army of Northern Virginia.

—Letter to General Lee dated April 7, 1865

General Lee was dressed in a full uniform, which was entirely new, and was wearing a sword of considerable value, very likely the sword which had been presented by the State of Virginia; at all events, it was an entirely different sword from the one that would ordinarily be worn in the field. In my rough traveling suit, the uniform of a private with the straps of a lieutenant-general, I must have contrasted very strangely with a man so handsomely dressed, six feet high and of faultless form. But this was not a matter that I thought of until afterwards.

—On the meeting with General Robert E. Lee at Appomattox Court House April 9, 1865

What General Lee's feelings were I do not know. As he was a man of much dignity, with an impassible face, it was impossible to say whether he felt inwardly glad that the end had finally come, or felt sad over the result, and was too manly to show it. Whatever his feelings, they were entirely concealed from my observation; but my own feelings, which had been quite jubilant on the receipt of his letter, were sad and depressed. I felt like anything rather than rejoicing at the downfall of a foe who had fought so long and valiantly, and had suffered so much for a cause, though that cause was, I believe, one of the worst for which a people ever fought, and one for which there was the least excuse. I do not question, however, the sincerity of the great mass of those who were opposed to us.

—On the meeting with General Robert E. Lee at Appomattox Court House April 9, 1865

No conversation, not one word, passed between General Lee and myself, either about private property, side arms, or kindred subjects. He appeared to have no objections to the terms first proposed; or if he had a point to make against them he wished to wait until they were in writing to make it. When he read over that part of the terms about side arms, horses and private property of the officers, he remarked, with some feeling, I thought, that this would have a happy effect upon his army. Lee and I then separated as cordially as we had met, he returning to his own lines, and all went into bivouac for the night at Appomattox. When news of the surrender first reached our lines our men commenced firing a salute of a hundred guns in honor of the victory. I at once sent word, however, to have it stopped. The Confederates were now our prisoners, and we did not want to exult over their downfall.

—About when the war ended

Name _____

Grant's Memoirs—Divided Reading

Part 1

On the anxiety that he felt prior to his first possible engagement as regiment commander during the Civil War

It occurred to me at once that Harris had been as much afraid of me as I had been of him. This was a view of the question I had never taken before; but it was one I never forgot afterwards. From that event to the close of the war, I never experienced trepidation upon confronting an enemy, though I always felt more or less anxiety. I never forgot that he had as much reason to fear my forces as I had his. The lesson was valuable.

Part 2

On the Battle of Shiloh

I saw an open field, in our possession on the second day, over which the Confederates had made repeated charges the day before, so covered with dead that it would have been possible to walk across the clearing, in any direction, stepping on dead bodies, without a foot touching the ground. The enemy fought bravely, but they had started out to defeat and destroy an army and capture a position. They failed in both, with very heavy loss in killed and wounded, and must have gone back discouraged and convinced that the "Yankee" was not an enemy to be despised.

Name _____

Grant's Memoirs—Divided Reading *(cont.)*

Part 3

Following the Battle of Champion's Hill

I always admired the South, as bad as I thought their cause, for the boldness with which they silenced all opposition and all croaking, by press or by individuals, within their control. War at all times, whether a civil war between sections of a common country or between nations, ought to be avoided, if possible with honor. But, once entered into, it is too much for human nature to tolerate an enemy within their ranks to give aid and comfort to the armies of the opposing section or nation. While a battle is raging one can see his enemy mowed down by the thousand, or the ten thousand, with great composure; but after the battle these scenes are distressing, and one is naturally disposed to do as much to alleviate the suffering of an enemy as a friend.

Part 4

On the Siege of Vicksburg

During the siege there had been a good deal of friendly sparring between the soldiers of the two armies, on picket and where the lines were close together. All rebels were known as "Johnnies," all Union troops as "Yanks." Often "Johnny" would call: "Well, Yank, when are you coming into town?" The reply was sometimes: "We propose to celebrate the 4th of July there." Sometimes it would be: "We always treat our prisoners with kindness and do not want to hurt them;" or, "We are holding you as prisoners of war while you are feeding yourselves." The garrison, from the commanding general down, undoubtedly expected an assault on the fourth. They knew from the temper of their men it would be successful when made; and that would be a greater humiliation than to surrender. Besides it would be attended with severe loss to them.

Name _____

Grant's Memoirs—Divided Reading (cont.)

Part 5

On the Siege of Vicksburg

At the appointed hour the garrison of Vicksburg marched out of their works and formed line in front, stacked arms and marched back in good order. Our whole army present witnessed this scene without cheering. Logan's division, which had approached nearest the rebel works, was the first to march in; and the flag of one of the regiments of his division was soon floating over the court-house. Our soldiers were no sooner inside the lines than the two armies began to fraternize. Our men had had full rations from the time the siege commenced, to the close. The enemy had been suffering, particularly towards the last. I myself saw our men taking bread from their haversacks and giving it to the enemy they had so recently been engaged in starving out. It was accepted with avidity and with thanks.

Part 6

About Abraham Lincoln

In my first interview with Mr. Lincoln alone he stated to me that he had never professed to be a military man or to know how campaigns should be conducted, and never wanted to interfere in them: but that procrastination on the part of commanders, and the pressure from the people at the North and Congress, WHICH WAS ALWAYS WITH HIM, forced him into issuing his series of "Military Orders"—one, two, three, etc. He did not know but they were all wrong, and did know that some of them were. All he wanted or had ever wanted was some one who would take the responsibility and act, and call on him for all the assistance needed, pledging himself to use all the power of the government in rendering such assistance. Assuring him that I would do the best I could with the means at hand, and avoid as far as possible annoying him or the War Department, our first interview ended. He always showed a generous and kindly spirit toward the Southern people, and I never heard him abuse an enemy. Some of the cruel things said about President Lincoln, particularly in the North, used to pierce him to the heart; but never in my presence did he evince a revengeful disposition.

Name _____

Grant's Memoirs—Divided Reading (cont.)

Part 7

Letter to General Lee dated April 7, 1865

The result of the last week must convince you of the hopelessness of further resistance on the part of the Army of Northern Virginia in this struggle. I feel that it is so, and regard it as my duty to shift from myself the responsibility of any further effusion of blood, by asking of you the surrender of that portion of the Confederate States army known as the Army of Northern Virginia.

Part 8

On the meeting with General Robert E. Lee at Appomattox Court House, April 9, 1865

General Lee was dressed in a full uniform, which was entirely new, and was wearing a sword of considerable value, very likely the sword which had been presented by the State of Virginia; at all events, it was an entirely different sword from the one that would ordinarily be worn in the field. In my rough traveling suit, the uniform of a private with the straps of a lieutenant-general, I must have contrasted very strangely with a man so handsomely dressed, six feet high and of faultless form. But this was not a matter that I thought of until afterwards.

Name _____

Grant's Memoirs—Divided Reading (cont.)

Part 9

On the meeting with General Robert E. Lee at Appomattox Court House, April 9, 1865

What General Lee's feelings were I do not know. As he was a man of much dignity, with an impassible face, it was impossible to say whether he felt inwardly glad that the end had finally come, or felt sad over the result, and was too manly to show it. Whatever his feelings, they were entirely concealed from my observation; but my own feelings, which had been quite jubilant on the receipt of his letter, were sad and depressed. I felt like anything rather than rejoicing at the downfall of a foe who had fought so long and valiantly, and had suffered so much for a cause, though that cause was, I believe, one of the worst for which a people ever fought, and one for which there was the least excuse. I do not question, however, the sincerity of the great mass of those who were opposed to us.

Part 10

About when the war ended

No conversation, not one word, passed between General Lee and myself, either about private property, side arms, or kindred subjects. He appeared to have no objections to the terms first proposed; or if he had a point to make against them he wished to wait until they were in writing to make it. When he read over that part of the terms about side arms, horses and private property of the officers, he remarked, with some feeling, I thought, that this would have a happy effect upon his army. Lee and I then separated as cordially as we had met, he returning to his own lines, and all went into bivouac for the night at Appomattox. When news of the surrender first reached our lines our men commenced firing a salute of a hundred guns in honor of the victory. I at once sent word, however, to have it stopped. The Confederates were now our prisoners, and we did not want to exult over their downfall.